GoodFood
magazine

101 CAKES & BAKES

First published 2004
Published by BBC Books, an imprint of Ebury Publishing
A Random House Group Company

30 29 28 27 26 25 24 23 22 21

Photographs © BBC Magazines 2004
Recipes © BBC Magazines 2004
Book design © Woodlands Books Ltd 2004
All the recipes contained in this book first appeared in
BBC Good Food Magazine.

The Random House Group Ltd Reg. No. 954009

Addresses for companies within the Random House Group Ltd can be
found at www.randomhouse.co.uk

A CIP catalogue record for this book is available from the British Library.

The Random House Group Limited supports The Forest Stewardship
Council (FSC), the leading international forest certification organisation.
All our titles that are printed on Greenpeace approved FSC certified
paper carry the FSC logo. Our paper procurement policy can be found
at www.rbooks.co.uk/environment

Commissioning Editor: Vivien Bowler
Project Editor: Warren Albers
Designers: Kathryn Gammon and Annette Peppis
Design Manager: Sarah Ponder
Production: Arlene Alexander

Set in Bookman Old Style, Helvetica and ITC Officina Sans
Printed and bound by Firmengruppe APPL, aprinta druck,
Wemding, Germany
Colour origination by Radstock Reproductions Ltd, Midsomer Norton

ISBN 978 0 563 52114 3

101 CAKES & BAKES
TRIED-AND-TESTED RECIPES

Editor
Mary Cadogan

BOOKS

Contents

Introduction

When the stresses of everyday life start to get to me, I find a session in the kitchen doing a bit of light cake making is the perfect answer. Cake making is sheer indulgence – nobody really needs a cake – though that's part of the pleasure. And the simple actions of beating together butter and sugar, folding in flour and rubbing mixtures together are enormously therapeutic.

Add to that the delicious smells that fill the house and the delight of all who share your baked offering, and the pleasure is complete. And whatever you make, it will always be a million times better than anything you could buy.

The cakes, biscuits and bakes in this book are all essentially very simple to make whether you are a beginner or an experienced baker, and you won't need loads of special equipment. You will find every cake you would ever want to make in these pages, from the classic recipes for shortbread and flapjacks, to exciting new ideas such as *Blueberry Cheesecake Gateau*, *Pumpkin and Ginger Teabread* and *Strawberry and Cinnamon Torte*.

So why wait? Get out your mixing bowl and spoon and get baking – you know it makes sense.

Mary Cadoga

Mary Cadogan
Food Director
BBC Good Food Magazine

Conversion tables

NOTES ON THE RECIPES

• Eggs are medium in the UK and Australia (large in America) unless stated otherwise.
• Wash all fresh produce before preparation.

OVEN TEMPERATURES

Gas	°C	Fan °C	°F	Oven temp.
¼	110	90	225	Very cool
½	120	100	250	Very cool
1	140	120	275	Cool or slow
2	150	130	300	Cool or slow
3	160	140	325	Warm
4	180	160	350	Moderate
5	190	170	375	Moderately hot
6	200	180	400	Fairly hot
7	220	200	425	Hot
8	230	210	450	Very hot
9	240	220	475	Very hot

APPROXIMATE WEIGHT CONVERSIONS

• All the recipes in this book list both imperial and metric measurements. Conversions are approximate and have been rounded up or down. Follow one set of measurements only; do not mix the two.
• Cup measurements, which are used by cooks in Australia and America, have not been listed here as they vary from ingredient to ingredient. Please use kitchen scales to measure dry/solid ingredients.

SPOON MEASURES
- Spoon measurements are level unless otherwise specified.
- 1 teaspoon = 5ml
- 1 tablespoon = 15ml
- 1 Australian tablespoon = 20ml (cooks in Australia should measure 3 teaspoons where 1 tablespoon is specified in a recipe)

APPROXIMATE LIQUID CONVERSIONS

metric	imperial	AUS	US
50ml	2fl oz	¼ cup	¼ cup
125ml	4fl oz	½ cup	½ cup
175ml	6fl oz	¾ cup	¾ cup
225ml	8fl oz	1 cup	1 cup
300ml	10fl oz/½ pint	½ pint	1¼ cups
450ml	16fl oz	2 cups	2 cups/1 pint
600ml	20fl oz/1 pint	1 pint	2½ cups
1 litre	35fl oz/1¾ pints	1¾ pints	1 quart

A special-occasion cake from *Good Food* reader
and baker Carrie Hill.

Cherry and Marzipan Cake

200g/8oz butter, softened
200g/8oz caster sugar
4 eggs, beaten
200g/8oz self-raising flour
200g/8oz glacé cherries, chopped
100g/4oz ground almonds
2–3 drops almond extract
250g/9oz marzipan
50g/2oz blanched almonds,
halved lengthways
icing sugar, for dusting

Takes 1 hour 55 minutes • Serves 12

1 Preheat the oven to 160°C/Gas 3/fan oven 140°C. Butter and line a deep 20cm/8in round cake tin. Beat the butter and sugar in a bowl until light and creamy. Pour in the eggs a little at a time and beat well after each addition. Mix in the flour one third at a time.
2 Fold in the cherries, ground almonds and almond extract until evenly mixed. Spoon half the mixture into the tin.
3 Roll out the marzipan to a 19cm/7½in circle. Lay this on top of the cake mixture in the tin, then cover with the rest of the mixture. Level, and scatter the almonds on top.
4 Bake for 1½ hours, or until a skewer inserted comes out clean, covering with foil after 1 hour. Leave to cool in the tin for 20 minutes, then turn out on to a wire rack and cool completely. Dust with icing sugar.

• Per serving 479 kcalories, protein 8g, carbohydrate 57g, fat 26g, saturated fat 10g, fibre 2g, added sugar 35g, salt 0.57g

This cake is based on a recipe by food writer Geraldene Holt,
who lived in Devon for many years.

Devonshire Honey Cake

225g/8oz unsalted butter
250g/9oz clear honey, plus about
2 tbsp extra to glaze
100g/4oz dark muscovado sugar
3 large eggs, beaten
300g/10oz self-raising flour

Takes 1½ hours • Serves 12

1 Preheat the oven to 160°C/Gas 3/fan oven 140°C. Butter and line a 20cm/8in round loose-bottomed cake tin. Cut the butter into pieces and drop into a medium pan with the honey and sugar. Melt slowly over a low heat. When liquid, increase the heat under the pan and boil for about one minute. Leave to cool.
2 Beat the eggs into the cooled honey mixture using a wooden spoon. Sift the flour into a large bowl and pour in the egg and honey mixture, beating until you have a smooth batter.
3 Pour the mixture into the tin and bake for 50 minutes–1 hour until the cake is well-risen, golden brown and springs back when pressed.
4 Turn the cake out on a wire rack. Warm 2 tablespoons of honey in a small pan and brush over the top of the cake to glaze, then leave to cool.

• Per serving 336 kcalories, protein 4g, carbohydrate 43g, fat 17g, saturated fat 10g, fibre 1g, added sugar 25g, salt 0.29g

Chuck the lot into a bowl, give it a quick beat
and it's ready to bake.

Cinnamon Nutella Cake

175g/6oz butter, softened
175g/6oz golden caster sugar
3 eggs
200g/8oz self-raising flour
1 tsp baking powder
2 tsp ground cinnamon
4 tbsp milk
4 rounded tbsp chocolate hazelnut spread
50g/2oz hazelnuts, roughly chopped

Takes 1½ hours • Serves 12

1 Preheat the oven to 180°C/Gas 4/fan oven 160°C. Butter and line the base of a 20cm/8in round cake tin.
2 Put the butter, sugar, eggs, flour, baking powder, cinnamon and milk into a bowl. Beat until light and fluffy.
3 Tip three quarters of the mixture into the tin, spread it level, then spoon the hazelnut spread on in four blobs. Top with the remaining mixture, swirl a few times with a skewer, then smooth.
4 Sprinkle with the nuts. Bake for 1 hour–1 hour 10 minutes, until risen, nicely browned, feels firm to the touch and springs back when lightly pressed (cover with foil if it starts to brown too quickly). Cool in the tin for 10 minutes, then turn out, peel off the paper and cool on a wire rack.

• Per serving 320 kcalories, protein 5g, carbohydrate 34g, fat 19g, saturated fat 8g, fibre 1g, added sugar 20g, salt 0.63g

Remind yourself of the lovely moist flavour of coconut with this nostalgic bake.

Coconut Cake

175g/6oz butter, softened
175g/6oz golden caster sugar
175g/6oz self-raising flour
1½ tsp baking powder
3 eggs, beaten
50g/2oz desiccated coconut
2 tbsp coconut cream, or single cream

FOR THE BUTTERCREAM FILLING AND TOPPING
280g/10oz icing sugar
100g/4oz butter, softened
3 tbsp coconut cream, or single cream
5 tbsp raspberry jam

Takes 45 minutes • Serves 8

1 Preheat the oven to 180°C/Gas 4/fan oven 160°C. Butter two 20cm/8in sandwich tins and line the bases with greaseproof paper. Mix the butter, sugar, flour, baking powder and eggs in a food processor for 2–3 minutes until smooth. Gently stir in the coconut and cream.
2 Divide the mixture between the tins and smooth the tops. Bake for 25 minutes until evenly golden and firm. Loosen the edges and leave in the tins for 5 minutes, then turn out on to a wire rack to cool. Peel off the lining paper.
3 Make the buttercream: beat together the icing sugar, butter and coconut cream until smooth. Spread one sponge with the jam. Top with just under half the buttercream and sandwich with the other sponge. Swirl the remaining buttercream on top of the cake.

• Per serving 410 kcalories, protein 9g, carbohydrate 42g, fat 23g, saturated fat 13g, fibre 1g, added sugar 14g, salt 1.22g

This egg-free cake is a real teatime treat – it's packed with fruit and cinnamon.

Carrot, Apple and Raisin Cake

225g/8oz self-raising flour
½ tsp baking powder
½ tsp salt
1 tsp ground cinnamon
5 tbsp vegetable oil
grated zest of 1 orange plus
4 tbsp juice
140g/5oz light muscovado sugar
140g/5oz finely grated carrot
1 medium eating apple, peeled,
cored and grated
85g/3oz raisins
50g/2oz pumpkin seeds
icing sugar, for dusting

Takes 1 hour 40 minutes • Serves 12

1 Preheat the oven to 180°C/Gas 4/fan oven 160°C. Butter a 20cm/8in round cake tin. Mix the flour, baking powder, salt and cinnamon together in a large bowl. In a separate bowl mix together the oil, orange juice and sugar.
2 Add the orange mixture to the flour along with the grated carrot and apple, orange zest, raisins and pumpkin seeds and stir until really well mixed. Spoon into the prepared tin.
3 Bake for 50 minutes–1 hour, until the cake pulls from the side of the tin. Cool on a rack before removing from tin. Dust with icing sugar and serve.

• Per serving 207 kcalories, protein 3g, carbohydrate 36g, fat 7g, saturated fat 1g, fibre 1g, added sugar 13g, salt 0.47g

This traditional cake for Guy Fawkes' night
will keep for up to two weeks.

Authentic Yorkshire Parkin

1 egg
3 tbsp milk
175g/6oz golden syrup
100g/4oz black treacle
85g/3oz light muscovado sugar
225g/8oz butter
100g/4oz medium oatmeal
250g/9oz plain flour
2 rounded tsp ground ginger
2 tsp bicarbonate of soda

Takes 1 hour 10 minutes • Serves 16

1 Preheat the oven to 160°C/Gas 3/fan oven 140°C. Butter a deep 23cm/9in square cake tin and line. Beat the egg and stir in the milk, then set aside.
2 Put the syrup, treacle, sugar and butter in a large pan and heat gently until the sugar has dissolved and the butter has melted. Remove from the heat. Mix together the oatmeal, flour, ginger and bicarbonate of soda, then stir into the syrup mixture, followed by the egg and milk. Combine well.
3 Pour the mixture into the tin and bake for 50 minutes–1 hour until the cake feels firm and a little crusty on top. Leave to cool in the tin, then turn out and peel off the paper. Wrap the parkin in clean greaseproof paper and foil and leave it for at least three days – this allows it to become much softer and stickier.

• Per serving 261 kcalories, protein 3g, carbohydrate 36g, fat 13g, saturated fat 8g, fibre 1g, added sugar 18g, salt 0.38g

You can store this cake for up to a week in a tin.

Raisin Spice Cake

FOR THE TOPPING
25g/1oz butter
25g/1oz demerara sugar
1 tsp mixed spice
25g/1oz chopped nuts

FOR THE CAKE
175ml/6fl oz unsweetened orange juice
175g/6oz raisins
175g/6oz butter
175g/6oz light muscovado sugar
250g/9oz self-raising flour
1 tsp mixed spice
1 tsp ground cinnamon
1 tsp ground ginger
3 eggs, beaten

Takes 1 hour 20 minutes •
Serves 10–12

1 Preheat the oven to 160°C/Gas 3/fan oven 140°C. Butter a 23cm/9in ring tin or 20cm/8in round cake tin. Make the topping: chop the butter into the topping ingredients, then sprinkle in the tin.
2 Pour the juice into a pan, then add the raisins, butter and sugar. Bring to the boil, stirring, then simmer for 5 minutes.
3 Lift off the heat; cool for 10 minutes. Sift the flour, mixed spice, cinnamon and ginger into the pan, then add the eggs and mix. Pour into the tin and smooth the top.
4 Bake for 45 minutes until firm. Cool in the tin for 5 minutes, then transfer on to a wire rack to cool completely.

• Per serving (for ten) 408 kcalories, protein 6g, carbohydrate 54g, fat 20g, saturated fat 11g, fibre 1g, added sugar 20g, salt 0.75g

A lovely moist cake that gets even better if left undisturbed
in the cake tin for a couple of days.

Porter Cake

175g/6oz butter
450g/1lb mixed dried fruit
grated zest and juice of 1 orange
175g/6oz light muscovado sugar
200ml/7fl oz porter, Guinness or
Caffrey's
1 tsp bicarbonate of soda
3 eggs, beaten
300g/10oz plain flour
2 tsp mixed spice

FOR THE TOPPING
2 tbsp flaked almonds
2 tbsp demerara sugar

Takes 2 hours 25 minutes • Serves 12

1 Preheat the oven to 150°C/Gas 2/fan oven 130°C. Butter and line the base of a deep 20cm/8in round cake tin. Put the butter, dried fruit, orange zest and juice, sugar and porter in a large pan. Bring slowly to the boil, stirring until the butter has dissolved, then simmer for 15 minutes.
2 Cool for 10 minutes, then stir in the bicarbonate of soda. The mixture will foam up, but don't worry, this is normal.
3 Stir the eggs into the pan, then sift in the flour and spice and mix well. Pour into the prepared tin, smooth the top with the back of a spoon and sprinkle with the flaked almonds and demerara sugar. Bake for 1¼–1½ hours. Cool in the tin for 15 minutes, then turn out and cool on a wire rack.

• Per serving 400 kcalories, protein 6g, carbohydrate 63g, fat 15g, saturated fat 8g, fibre 2g, added sugar 17g, salt 0.69g

You can make the cake a couple of days in advance,
wrap well, then ice on the day of serving.

Sticky Ginger Cake with Ginger Fudge Icing

200g/8oz unsalted butter, diced
175g/6oz molasses sugar
3 tbsp black treacle
150ml/¼ pint milk
2 large eggs, beaten
4 pieces stem ginger, drained from
their syrup, chopped
300g/10oz self-raising flour
1 tbsp ground ginger

FOR THE ICING
4 tbsp ginger syrup, drained from jar
300g/10oz golden icing sugar, sifted
140g/5oz unsalted butter, softened
2 tsp lemon juice

Takes 1 hour 10 minutes • Serves 16

1 Preheat the oven to 160°C/Gas 3/fan oven 140°C. Butter and line the base of a 23cm/9in round cake tin. Gently melt the butter, sugar and treacle; cool briefly, then stir in the milk. Beat in the eggs and add the chopped stem ginger. Sift the flour, ground ginger and a pinch of salt into the warm mixture. Combine thoroughly.
2 Spoon the cake mixture into the tin and level the surface. Bake for 30–35 minutes or until firm and risen. Cool in the tin for an hour, then transfer to a wire rack.
3 Skewer the top of the cooled cake all over, then pour 2 tablespoons of the syrup over. Beat together the icing sugar, butter, lemon juice and the remaining ginger syrup, and spread over the cake.

• Per serving 379 kcalories, protein 3g, carbohydrate 53g, fat 19g, saturated fat 11g, fibre 1g, added sugar 37g, salt 0.27g

Light and enticingly moist, this cake keeps
for up to a week in a tin.

Yummy Scrummy Carrot Cake

175g/6oz light muscovado sugar
175ml/6fl oz sunflower oil
3 large eggs, lightly beaten
140g/5oz grated carrot (about
3 medium carrots)
100g/4oz raisins
grated zest of 1 large orange
175g/6oz self-raising flour
1 tsp bicarbonate of soda
1 tsp ground cinnamon
½ tsp grated nutmeg (freshly grated
will give you the best flavour)

FOR THE FROSTING
175g/6oz icing sugar
1½–2 tbsp orange juice

Takes 1¼ hours • Serves 15

1 Preheat the oven to 180°C/Gas 4/fan
oven 160°C. Oil and line the base and sides
of an 18cm/7in square cake tin. Tip the
sugar into a large mixing bowl, pour in the oil
and add the eggs. Lightly mix, then stir in the
grated carrots, raisins and orange rind.
2 Mix the flour, soda and spices, then sift
into the bowl. Lightly mix all the ingredients.
3 Pour the mixture into the prepared tin and
bake for 40–45 minutes, until it feels firm and
springy when you press it in the centre. Cool
in the tin for 5 minutes, then turn it out, peel
off the paper and cool on a wire rack.
4 Beat together the frosting ingredients in a
small bowl until smooth. Set the cake on a
serving plate and drizzle the icing over the
top. Leave to set, then cut into slices.

• Per serving 265 kcalories, protein 3g, carbohydrate
39g, fat 12g, saturated fat 2g, fibre 1g, added sugar
24g, salt 0.41g

The flavour of the olive oil comes through along with the citrus fruits and the almonds.

Olive Oil Cake

1 orange
1 lemon
4 large eggs
115g/4oz caster sugar
175g/6oz plain flour
1 tbsp baking powder
225ml/8fl oz extra virgin olive oil
100g/4oz blanched almonds,
toasted and finely chopped
icing sugar, for dusting

Takes 1 hour 25 minutes • Serves 12

1 Preheat the oven to 180°C/Gas 4/fan oven 160°C. Oil and line the base of a 23cm/9in loose-bottomed or springform round cake tin. Put the orange and lemon in a pan and cover with water. Bring to the boil and leave to simmer for 30 minutes until very soft. Drain and cool. Cut away the skin from the white pith and whizz the skin to a puréed paste in a food processor.
2 In a large bowl, beat the eggs with the sugar for 7–8 minutes. Sift the flour, baking powder and a pinch of salt together, then fold lightly into the egg mixture along with the olive oil. Very gently fold in the almonds and puréed fruit skin, but don't overmix.
3 Pour the batter into the tin and bake for 45 minutes. Cool on a wire rack, then dust with icing sugar.

• Per serving 333 kcalories, protein 6g, carbohydrate 25g, fat 24g, saturated fat 3g, fibre 1g, added sugar 11g, salt 0.45g

Stays soft and moist in the middle, and the icing
sets to a crisp meringue-like coating.

Pecan Ginger Cake

200g/8oz self-raising flour
4 tsp ground ginger
1 tsp baking powder
½ tsp salt
200g/8oz butter
350g/12oz golden syrup
100g/4oz light muscovado sugar
4 eggs, beaten
100g/4oz pecans, roughly chopped
100g/4oz crystallized ginger,
chopped

FOR THE TOPPING AND DECORATION
175g/6oz golden granulated sugar
1 egg white
pinch of cream of tartar
85g/3oz sugar
100g/4oz pecan halves

Takes 1 hour • Serves 10

1 Preheat the oven to 180°C/Gas 4/fan oven 160°C. Butter and line the base of two 20cm/8in cake tins. Sift together the flour, ginger, baking powder and salt. Rub in the butter until it resembles crumbs.

2 Beat in the syrup, sugar, eggs, pecans and ginger. Pour into the tins and bake for 45 minutes until firm. Cool in the tins for 10 minutes, then turn out on to a wire rack.

3 Put the golden sugar, egg white, cream of tartar and 2 tablespoons hot water in a bowl set over (not in) a pan of simmering water. Beat for 10 minutes. Layer the cakes with a little icing; swirl the rest over the top and sides.

4 Heat the sugar with four tablespoons of water until dissolved, then boil until it forms a caramel. Stir in the pecan halves, cool on an oiled baking sheet, then use to decorate.

• Per serving 659 kcalories, protein 7g, carbohydrate 90g, fat 33g, saturated fat 11g, fibre 2g, added sugar 43g, salt 1.3g

It's big, it's rich, it's moist – and impossible to resist.

Mocha Fudge Cake with Coffee Icing

FOR THE ICING
175g/6oz plain chocolate, melted
50g/2oz unsalted butter, melted
150ml/¼ pint double-strength espresso
1 tsp vanilla extract
300g/10oz icing sugar

FOR THE CAKE
300g/10oz plain flour, plus extra
2 tsp baking powder
1 tsp vanilla extract
3 eggs, separated
125ml/4fl oz milk
4 tbsp instant coffee granules
85g/3oz unsalted butter
280g/10oz caster sugar
85g/3oz plain chocolate, melted
125ml/4fl oz soured cream

Takes 1 hour 5 minutes, plus 4 hours chilling • Serves 10

1 Whisk together the cooled icing ingredients. Cover and chill for 3–4 hours.
2 Preheat the oven to 180ºC/Gas 4/fan oven 160ºC. Butter and flour two 20cm/8in cake tins. Sift the flour and baking powder. Stir the vanilla into the egg yolks. Heat half the milk to boiling point, stir in the coffee to dissolve, then add the rest of the milk and cool.
3 Cream the butter and 200g/8oz of the caster sugar. Slowly whisk in the egg yolk mixture, then the melted chocolate. Fold in the sifted dry ingredients, the cooled milk and the soured cream. Whisk the egg whites until stiff; whisk in the remaining sugar to form firm peaks. Fold the egg whites into the cake mixture and pour into the tins. Bake for 30 minutes until risen. Cool, split each cake in two, and layer with the icing.

• Per serving 627 kcalories, protein 8g, carbohydrate 103g, fat 23g, saturated fat 13g, fibre 2g, added sugar 77g, salt 0.42g

This tall cake is spectacular, easy to make and
keeps for up to one day in the fridge.

Blueberry Cheesecake Gateau

225g/9oz self-raising flour
1 tsp baking powder
200g/8oz caster sugar
200g/8oz butter, softened
4 large eggs
2 tsp vanilla extract
1 tbsp milk

FOR THE ICING AND DECORATION
400g/14oz medium-fat soft cheese
grated zest of 2 limes and the
juice of 1
100g/4oz icing sugar
200g/8oz blueberries

Takes 1¼ hours, plus 30 minutes
decorating • Serves 12

1 Preheat the oven to 180°C/Gas 4/fan
oven 160°C. Butter and line the base of
a deep 18cm/7in round cake tin.
2 Put the flour, baking powder, sugar, butter,
eggs and vanilla into a large bowl and beat
with an electric mixer on low speed until
everything is mixed together. Increase the
speed and whisk for 2 minutes. Stir in the milk.
3 Spoon the mixture into the tin and level the
top. Bake the cake for about 50–60 minutes,
until the cake springs back when lightly
pressed, cool, then split into three layers.
4 Beat the cheese until soft, then beat in
the lime zest and juice and the icing sugar.
Sandwich the cake back together with two
thirds of the cheese mixture, and spread the
rest on the top. Arrange the blueberries in
tight circles around the top of the cake.

• Per serving 380 kcalories, protein 8g, carbohydrate
43g, fat 21g, saturated fat 9g, fibre 1g, added sugar
27g, salt 0.69g

Make this cake the day before a picnic – it's sturdy and travels well.

Fresh Cherry Cake with a Hint of Cinnamon

140g/5oz self-raising flour
½ tsp ground cinnamon
50g/2oz golden caster sugar
1 egg
4 tbsp milk
85g/3oz butter, melted
350g/12oz juicy, ripe cherries, stalks and stones removed
icing sugar, for dusting

FOR THE TOPPING
25g/1oz plain flour
¼ tsp ground cinnamon
25g/1oz golden caster sugar
25g/1oz butter, diced and softened

Takes 1 hour 5 minutes • Serves 8

1 Preheat the oven to 180°C/Gas 4/fan oven 160°C. Butter and line the base of a 20cm/8in round cake tin. Sift the flour, cinnamon and sugar into a bowl. Make a well and add the egg, milk and melted butter. Combine and beat to make a thick, smooth mixture. Spoon into the tin and smooth. Scatter the cherries over the mixture and gently press them in.

2 Tip all the topping ingredients into a bowl. Rub in the butter to make a crumb-like mixture, then work until it comes together in pea-sized pieces. Scatter this over the cherries.

3 Bake for 30–35 minutes until a skewer pushed into the centre comes out clean. Leave in the tin until cool enough to handle, then tip on to a wire rack until completely cold.

• Per serving 247 kcalories, protein 3g, carbohydrate 32g, fat 12g, saturated fat 7g, fibre 1g, added sugar 12g, salt 0.46g

This is good warm, as a pudding with whipped cream,
or cold, as a moist fruity cake.

Rhubarb and Orange Cake

350g/12oz prepared rhubarb, cut into 4cm/1½in lengths
200g/8oz golden caster sugar
finely grated zest and juice of ½ small orange
140g/5oz butter, softened
2 eggs, beaten
½ tsp baking powder
85g/3oz self-raising flour
100g/4oz ground almonds

FOR THE TOPPING
25g/1oz butter, melted
25g/1oz light muscovado sugar
finely grated zest of ½ small orange
50g/2oz slivered almonds
icing sugar, for dusting

Takes 1 hour 25 minutes, plus 1 hour standing • Serves 6–8

1 Mix the rhubarb with 50g/2oz of the caster sugar and the orange zest. Set aside for 1 hour, stirring once or twice.
2 Preheat the oven to 190°C/Gas 5/fan oven 170°C. Butter and line the base of a deep 23cm/9in round cake tin. Cream the butter and remaining caster sugar. Add the eggs, baking powder, flour and ground almonds. Beat gently, but do not overmix. Stir in the orange juice, spoon into the tin, and level. Drain the rhubarb and spoon over the mixture. Bake for 25 minutes. Meanwhile, combine the butter, sugar, zest and almonds.
3 Reduce the oven to 180°C/Gas 4/fan oven 160°C. Sprinkle the topping over the cake and return to the oven for 15–20 minutes or until firm. Cool in the tin, then transfer to a rack. Dust with icing sugar.

• Per serving (for six) 548 kcalories, protein 9g, carbohydrate 44g, fat 39g, saturated fat 16g, fibre 3g, added sugar 41g, salt 0.74g

This cake conjures up the taste of the Caribbean.

St Lucia Banana Cake

350g/12oz self-raising flour
1 tsp bicarbonate of soda
2 tsp mixed spice
175g/6oz light muscovado sugar
4 eggs
200ml/7fl oz sunflower oil
2 bananas, mashed
100g/4oz pineapple, very finely chopped
finely grated rind and juice of 1 orange
100g pack walnuts, roughly chopped

FOR THE FROSTING
2 × 200g packs medium-fat soft cheese, at room temperature
200g/8oz icing sugar
50g/2oz honey-coated banana chips

Takes 1 hour 5 minutes • Serves 12

1 Preheat the oven to 180°C/Gas 4/fan oven 160°C. Butter and line two 20cm/8in sandwich tins. Sift the flour into a large bowl with the soda, mixed spice and sugar.

2 Whisk the eggs and the oil until smooth. Stir the egg mixture into the flour with the bananas, pineapple, orange rind and juice and walnuts; stir well. Divide between the prepared tins. Bake for 45 minutes until risen and firm. Cool for 10 minutes, then remove from the tins, peel off the paper and leave to cool completely.

3 Beat the soft cheese until smooth. Gradually add the icing sugar to give a smooth frosting. Spread half the frosting over one cake. Put the other cake on top. Spread over the remaining icing, swirling it with a palette knife. Sprinkle over the banana chips.

• Per serving 545 kcalories, protein 10g, carbohydrate 64g, fat 30g, saturated fat 3g, fibre 2g, added sugar 32g, salt 0.66g

A bold, unusual dessert that marries fruit and herbs.

Lemon Polenta Cake with Rosemary Syrup

175g/6oz polenta
50g/2oz plain flour
1½ tsp baking powder
¼ tsp salt
5 tbsp natural yogurt
5 tbsp groundnut oil, plus extra for greasing
grated rind of 2 lemons, plus 2 tbsp fresh lemon juice
2 eggs, plus 2 egg whites
400g/14oz caster sugar
2 sprigs fresh rosemary, plus extra sprigs to decorate
fresh raspberries and Greek yogurt, to serve

Takes 1 hour 5 minutes • Serves 8–10

1 Preheat the oven to 180°C/Gas 4/fan oven 160°C. Sift the polenta, flour, baking powder and salt into a bowl. Tip the yogurt, oil, lemon rind and juice into a jug; stir to combine.
2 Beat the eggs and egg whites with half the sugar until creamy. Beat in the yogurt mixture until smooth, then fold in the dry ingredients. Pour the batter into a 1.2 litre/2 pint lightly oiled, lined loaf tin. Bake for 40–45 minutes or until a skewer inserted comes out clean.
3 Put the remaining sugar in a pan with 200ml/7fl oz of water and the rosemary sprigs. Bring to the boil, then simmer for 10 minutes. Cool completely, then strain.
4 Cool the cake on a wire rack for 15 minutes. Prick the top and drizzle over half the rosemary syrup. Serve with the rosemary sprigs, raspberries, yogurt and extra syrup.

• Per serving (for eight) 390 kcalories, protein 6g, carbohydrate 74g, fat 10g, saturated fat 2g, fibre 1g, added sugar 53g, salt 0.43g

This crumbly cake is a terrific way to enjoy fresh cherries.

Fresh Cherry Almond Cake

140g/5oz whole blanched almonds
250g/9oz self-raising flour
140g/5oz butter, cut into small
pieces and softened
140g/5oz caster sugar
2 eggs, beaten
125ml/4fl oz milk
300g/10oz fresh cherries, stoned
and patted dry
25g/1oz flaked almonds

Takes 1½ hours • Serves 8

1 Preheat the oven to 180°C/Gas 4/fan oven 160°C. Butter and line the base of a 20cm/8in round, deep cake tin. Put the blanched almonds in a small pan and heat gently, shaking occasionally, until golden brown (about 10 minutes). Cool, then whizz in a food processor until finely ground.
2 Tip the flour into a bowl and stir in the ground almonds. Rub in the butter until the mixture is crumbly. Stir in the sugar, then add the eggs, milk and cherries; mix until combined, but don't overmix.
3 Spoon into the prepared tin and smooth the top, then sprinkle the flaked almonds on top. Bake for 1 hour 10 minutes until the cake is golden on top and firm to the touch. Cool in the tin for 10 minutes, then turn out on to a wire rack to cool. Eat within 3 days.

• Per serving 474 kcalories, protein 10g, carbohydrate 48g, fat 28g, saturated fat 11g, fibre 2.8g, added sugar 18g, salt 0.69g

Serve this warm from the oven as a tasty dessert,
or cold for a picnic or lunchbox treat.

Apple and Cinnamon Cake

250g/9oz self-raising flour
1 tsp ground cinnamon
1 tsp baking powder
100g/4oz light muscovado sugar
175g/6oz sultanas or raisins
125ml/4fl oz sunflower oil
2 eggs, beaten
125ml/4fl oz apple juice
2 dessert apples (not peeled), grated
25g/1oz slivered or flaked almonds
icing sugar, for dusting

Takes 1 hour • Serves 8–10

1 Preheat the oven to 180°C/Gas 4/fan oven 160°C. Line a 23cm/9in round deep cake tin with baking paper. Sift the flour into a bowl with the cinnamon and baking powder, then stir in the sugar and sultanas. Make a well in the centre and stir in the oil, eggs, apple juice and grated apple until well mixed.
2 Pour the mixture into the tin, scatter with almonds, then bake for 40–45 minutes until firm in the centre or a skewer inserted into the middle comes out clean. Leave to cool in the tin for about 5 minutes, then turn out and cool on a wire rack. Dust with icing sugar.

• Per serving (for ten) 342 kcalories, protein 6g, carbohydrate 46g, fat 16g, saturated fat 2g, fibre 2g, added sugar 10g, salt 0.46g

Wonderfully moist and fruity, this cake is a teatime favourite.

Raspberry and Blueberry Lime Drizzle Cake

225g/8oz butter, softened
225g/8oz golden caster sugar
4 eggs
250g/9oz self-raising flour, sifted with
a pinch of salt
grated zest and juice of 2 limes
25g/1oz ground almonds
100g/4oz each blueberries and
raspberries

FOR THE SYRUP
8 tbsp lime juice (about 4 limes)
grated zest of 1 lime
140g/5oz golden caster sugar

Takes 1 hour and 25 minutes •
Serves 12

1 Preheat the oven to 180°C/Gas 4/fan oven 160°C. Line the base and sides of a 20cm/8in square cake tin and butter the paper.
2 Cream the butter and sugar together until light. Gradually beat in the eggs, adding a little of the flour towards the end to prevent curdling. Beat in the lime zest, then fold in the rest of the flour and almonds. Fold in about 3 tablespoons of lime juice, giving a good dropping consistency. Fold in three quarters of the blueberries and raspberries and turn into the prepared tin. Smooth, then scatter the remaining fruit on top. Bake for about 1 hour or until firm.
3 Gently heat the lime juice, zest and sugar in a saucepan, without allowing to bubble. While the cake is still hot, prick it all over with a skewer then spoon the syrup over it.

• Per serving 370 kcalories, protein 5g, carbohydrate 49g, fat 19g, saturated fat 10g, fibre 1g, added sugar 32g, salt 0.61g

This cake is very moist and light, and the apricots add a juicy note –
a brilliant special-occasion dessert.

Almond Cake with Clementines

100g/4oz ready-to-eat dried apricots
175ml/6fl oz clementine juice (about
6–8 clementines)
100g/4oz butter, softened
100g/4oz golden caster sugar
2 eggs
50g/2oz self-raising flour
175g/6oz ground almonds
½ tsp vanilla extract
2 tbsp slivered almonds
icing sugar, for dusting
8 clementines in syrup (from a jar),
to serve
thick cream or Greek yogurt,
to serve

Takes 1 hour 50 minutes • Serves 8

1 Preheat the oven to 180°C/Gas 4/fan oven 160°C. Butter and line the base of a 20cm/8in round cake tin. Finely chop the apricots and put in a pan with the clementine juice. Bring to the boil, then gently simmer for 5 minutes. Leave to cool.

2 Beat the butter, sugar, eggs and flour in a bowl for 2 minutes until light and fluffy, then fold in the ground almonds, vanilla and apricots along with their juices.

3 Turn the mixture into the prepared tin and smooth. Scatter the slivered almonds on top. Bake for 40–50 minutes until firm. Cool in the tin for 5 minutes, then turn out and cool on a wire rack. Dust the cake with icing sugar. Slice, and put a wedge on each plate with a clementine. Spoon the syrup over the cake and fruit. Serve with the cream or yogurt.

• Per serving 291 kcalories, protein 6g, carbohydrate 27g, fat 19g, saturated fat 8g, fibre 2g, added sugar 15g, salt 0.36g

Buy your mangos a couple of days ahead to ensure they are fully ripe.

Mango, Banana and Coconut Cake

1 medium, ripe mango
2 ripe bananas
1 tsp vanilla extract
225g/8oz butter, softened
140g/5oz light muscovado sugar
2 eggs, beaten
50g/2oz desiccated coconut
225g/8oz self-raising flour
½ tsp bicarbonate of soda
1 tsp mixed spice

FOR THE FILLING
200g packet full-fat soft cheese
2 tsp lemon juice
25g/1oz icing sugar, plus extra for dusting

Takes 55 minutes • Serves 10

1 Preheat the oven 160°C/Gas 3/fan oven 140°C. Butter and line the bases of two round 20cm/8in sandwich tins. Peel, stone and chop the mango, then purée the flesh. Mash the bananas, then mix in half the mango purée and the vanilla.
2 Beat together the butter and sugar until light and fluffy. Beat in the eggs, a little at a time, then stir in the banana mixture, and the coconut. Sift in the flour, bicarbonate of soda and spice, then fold in lightly. Divide the mixture between the tins and smooth. Bake for 30–35 minutes. Cool in the tins for 5 minutes, then turn out on to a wire rack.
3 Beat together the filling ingredients, then stir in the reserved mango. Spread one cake with the filling. Put the other cake on top and dust lightly with icing sugar.

• Per serving 468 kcalories, protein 5g, carbohydrate 42g, fat 32g, saturated fat 21g, fibre 2g, added sugar 17g, salt 0.83g

A perfect cake for Easter from Orlando Murrin,
editor of *Good Food Magazine*.

Lemon Flower Cake

FOR THE SUGAR-FROSTED FLOWERS
selection of pansies, calendulas and
other seasonal edible flowers
1 egg white, very lightly beaten
caster sugar, for coating the flowers

FOR THE CAKE
175g/6oz butter, softened
175g/6oz caster sugar
3 eggs
175g/6oz self-raising flour
1½ tsp baking powder
finely grated zest of 1 lemon

FOR THE TOPPING AND FILLING
85g/3oz caster sugar, plus extra for
sprinkling
juice of 1½ lemons
250g tub mascarpone

Takes 50 minutes, plus 2 hours drying
time • Serves 8–10

1 Brush the flower petals with the egg white,
then sprinkle with the caster sugar. Shake off
any excess. Leave for 2 hours to dry.
2 Preheat the oven to 190°C/Gas 5/fan oven
170°C. Lightly butter and line two 18cm/7in
round sandwich tins. Put all the cake
ingredients in a large mixing bowl, add a
tablespoon of warm water and beat until
smooth. Divide the mixture between the tins,
smooth, then bake for 25–30 minutes until the
cakes spring back when pressed.
3 Mix the topping sugar with the juice of one
lemon. Prick the cakes and spoon the topping
mixture over. Cool, then transfer to a wire rack.
Add the remaining lemon juice to the
mascarpone and use this mixture to layer the
cakes. Sprinkle caster sugar lightly over the
top, then decorate with the flowers.

• Per serving (for eight) 538 kcalories, protein 6g,
carbohydrate 54g, fat 35g, saturated fat 21g, fibre 1g,
added sugar 35g, salt 1.12g

This treat can be stored in the fridge for up to 3 days.

Citrus Poppy Seed Cake

175g/6oz butter, softened
175g/6oz caster sugar
3 eggs, beaten
250g/9oz self-raising flour
50g/2oz poppy seeds
grated rind of 2 oranges
grated rind of 2 lemons
4 rounded tbsp natural yogurt

FOR THE TOPPING
250g tub mascarpone
grated rind and juice of 1 small orange
3 tbsp orange or lemon curd
grated rind of 1 lemon

Takes 1 hour 5 minutes • Serves 10

1 Preheat the oven to 150°C/Gas 2/fan oven 130°C. Butter and line the base of a deep 20cm/8in round cake tin. Using a wooden spoon, beat together the butter, sugar, eggs, flour, poppy seeds, citrus rinds and yogurt until smooth.

2 Spread the mixture in the tin and bake for 45–50 minutes until just firm. Cool in the tin for 10 minutes, then turn out and cool on a wire rack. Peel off the paper.

3 Meanwhile, mix the mascarpone with enough orange juice to make a spreadable icing. Lightly swirl in the curd to give a marbled effect. Roughly spread over the top and sides of the cake, and scatter the grated citrus rind over the top to decorate.

• Per serving 483 kcalories, protein 7g, carbohydrate 48g, fat 31g, saturated fat 11g, fibre 2g, added sugar 18g, salt 0.74g

An all-in-one cake, topped with fresh apples,
then glazed for a beautiful finish.

Apple Cake in a Nutshell

3 eggs
175g/6oz butter, melted
350g/12oz self-raising flour
2 tsp ground cinnamon
175g/6oz light muscovado sugar
3 medium eating apples, such as
Cox's, unpeeled and cored
100g/4oz dates, stoned and cut
into pieces
100g/4oz blanched hazelnuts,
roughly chopped
3 tbsp apricot compote

Takes 1¼ hours • Serves 12

1 Preheat the oven to 180°C/Gas 4/fan oven 160°C. Butter and line the base of a 20cm/8in cake tin. Beat the eggs into the cooled butter. Put the flour, cinnamon and sugar into a separate bowl, and mix well.
2 Cut two of the apples into chunks. Stir the chunks into the flour with the dates and half of the hazelnuts. Mix well. Pour the egg and butter mixture into the flour mixture and stir gently. Spoon into the tin, and smooth.
3 Cut the remaining apple into thin slices and arrange over the cake. Sprinkle the remaining hazelnuts over the apple slices. Bake for 50 minutes–1 hour, or until a skewer inserted comes out clean. Cool in the tin for 5 minutes, then turn out on a wire rack. While the cake is still warm, heat the apricot compote. Brush over the cake, then cool completely.

• Per serving 377 kcalories, protein 6g, carbohydrate 49g, fat 19g, saturated fat 8g, fibre 3g, added sugar 15g, salt 0.61g

This unconventionally made bittersweet cake
freezes beautifully.

Orange and Almond Cake

1 medium orange
175g/6oz butter, softened
175g/6oz light muscovado sugar
3 eggs
175g/6oz self-raising flour
½ tsp bicarbonate of soda
50g/2oz ground almonds
icing sugar, for dredging

Takes 50 minutes • Serves 12

1 Preheat the oven to 190°C/Gas 5/fan oven 170°C. Butter and line the base of a 23cm/9in round deep cake tin. Cut the whole orange – skin, pith, flesh, the lot – into pieces. Remove any pips, then whizz the orange pieces in a food processor to a finely chopped purée.
2 Tip the butter, sugar, eggs, flour, bicarbonate of soda and almonds into the processor and whizz for 10 seconds, until smooth. Pour into the prepared tin and smooth the top.
3 Bake for 25–30 minutes, until the cake is risen and brown. Allow to cool in the tin for 5 minutes before turning out on to a wire rack. Dredge thickly with icing sugar before serving.

• Per serving 266 kcalories, protein 4g, carbohydrate 29g, fat 16g, saturated fat 8g, fibre 1g, added sugar 16g, salt 0.61g

These squares are really light, and delicious hot or cold.

Soured Cream Rhubarb Squares

100g/4oz butter, softened
100g/4oz golden caster sugar
100g/4oz mixed nuts, roughly
chopped
1 tsp ground cinnamon
250g/9oz dark muscovado sugar
1 large egg
225g/8oz plain flour
1 tsp bicarbonate of soda
½ tsp salt
2 × 142ml cartons soured cream
300g/10oz rhubarb, cut into 1cm
pieces

Takes 1 hour 20 minutes • Serves 15

1 Preheat the oven to 180°C/Gas 4/fan oven 160°C. Line a 33 × 23cm/13 × 9in deep baking tin with baking paper. Melt about 15g/½oz of the butter and stir into the caster sugar, nuts and cinnamon in a bowl. Set aside.

2 Beat together the rest of the butter with the muscovado sugar and egg. When smooth and creamy, stir in the flour, bicarbonate of soda, salt and the soured cream. Lastly, stir in the rhubarb.

3 Pour the rhubarb mixture into the prepared tin and sprinkle with the sugar and nut topping. Bake for 30–35 minutes or until a skewer inserted in the centre comes out clean. Serve immediately as a pudding, or leave to cool and cut into squares. Keeps for 4–5 days in an airtight tin.

• Per serving 277 kcalories, protein 4g, carbohydrate 37g, fat 13g, saturated fat 7g, fibre 1g, added sugar 24g, salt 0.63g

The perfect crumbly dessert for a summer
Sunday lunch or dinner.

Strawberry and Cinnamon Torte

175g/6oz ground almonds
175g/6oz butter, softened
175g/6oz golden caster sugar
175g/6oz self-raising flour
1 tsp ground cinnamon
1 egg, plus 1 egg yolk
450g/1lb strawberries, hulled and
sliced
icing sugar, for dusting
whipped double cream mixed with
Greek yogurt, to serve

Takes 1¼ hours • Serves 6–8

1 Preheat the oven to 180°C/Gas 4/fan oven 160°C. Butter and line the base of a loose-bottomed 23cm/9in cake tin. In a food processor, mix the ground almonds, butter, sugar, flour, cinnamon, egg and egg yolk until evenly mixed.
2 Tip half the mixture in the tin, and smooth. Spread the strawberries on top. Top with the remaining cake mixture; spread smooth.
3 Bake for 1 hour–1 hour 5 minutes. Check after 40 minutes – if the torte is getting too brown, cover loosely with foil. When cooked, the torte should be slightly risen and dark golden brown.
4 Cool slightly, then remove from the tin. Slide on to a plate and dust with icing sugar. Serve warm, in wedges, with spoonfuls of cream and Greek yogurt.

• Per serving (for eight) 491 kcalories, protein 9g, carbohydrate 45g, fat 32g, saturated fat 13g, fibre 3g, added sugar 23g, salt 0.68g

Blueberries bake really well in cakes, as their purple
skins keep in their juicy centres.

Blueberry Soured Cream Cake

175g/6oz butter, softened
175g/6oz golden caster sugar
3 large eggs
225g/8oz self-raising flour
1 tsp baking powder
2 tsp vanilla extract
142ml carton soured cream
3 × 125g punnets blueberries

FOR THE FROSTING
200g tub soft cheese (such as
Philadelphia)
100g/4oz icing sugar

Takes 1 hour 25 minutes • Serves 10

1 Preheat the oven to 180°C/Gas 4/fan
oven 160°C. Butter and line the base of a
23cm/9in round cake tin. Put the butter,
sugar, eggs, flour, baking powder and vanilla
in a bowl. Beat for 2–3 minutes until pale and
well mixed. Beat in 4 tablespoons soured
cream, then stir in half the blueberries.
2 Tip the mixture into the tin and level. Bake
for 50 minutes, or until it feels firm to the touch
and springs back when lightly pressed. Cool
for 10 minutes, then take out of the tin and
peel off the paper. Leave to finish cooling.
3 Beat the soft cheese with the icing sugar
and the remaining soured cream until smooth
and creamy. Spread over the top of the
cooled cake and scatter with the remaining
blueberries. The cake will keep in the fridge
for a couple of days.

• Per serving 469 kcalories, protein 6g, carbohydrate
50g, fat 29g, saturated fat 17g, fibre 1g, added sugar
29g, salt 0.93g

This tasty cake can be made in advance, but is best
eaten within 2–3 days.

Raspberry and Almond Madeira Cake

175g/6oz butter, softened
175g/6oz caster sugar
1 tsp vanilla extract
3 eggs, lightly beaten
50g/2oz flaked almonds
grated zest of 1 orange
100g/4oz plain flour, sifted
100g/4oz self-raising flour, sifted
2 tbsp milk
200g/8oz raspberries, fresh or frozen
icing sugar, for dusting

Takes 1½ hours • Serves 8

1 Preheat the oven to 160°C/Gas 3/fan oven 140°C. Line a deep 20cm/8in cake tin. Cream the butter and sugar. Beat in the vanilla, then gradually beat in the eggs.
2 Set aside a few almonds. Crumble the rest and stir them and the zest into the batter. Fold in the sifted flours and milk, then fold in all but eight of the raspberries.
3 Put the mixture in the tin and level, then arrange the remaining raspberries on top. Sprinkle the remaining almonds over the top, and bake for 1 hour 15 minutes. Cool in the tin for 10 minutes, then cool on a rack. Dust with icing sugar.

• Per serving 410 kcalories, protein 7g, carbohydrate 45g, fat 24g, saturated fat 12g, fibre 2g, added sugar 24g, salt 0.61g

The juicy flavour of a whole orange goes into this cake.

Whole Orange Cake

1 small orange
140g/5oz caster sugar
3 eggs
85g/3oz self-raising flour
100g/4oz ground almonds
50g/2oz butter, melted

FOR THE ICING
85g/3oz icing sugar
juice of 1 small sweet orange (or
enough to make a smooth
pouring icing)
crème fraîche, to serve (optional)

Takes 1 hour 45 minutes •
Serves 8–10

1 Put the orange in a pan and cover with cold water. Bring to the boil, cover and simmer for 1 hour. Remove the orange and cool.
2 Preheat the oven to 180°C/Gas 4/fan oven 160°C. Butter and line the base of a 20cm/8in round, deep cake tin. Roughly chop the cooked orange, discarding the pips. Whizz in a food processor until smooth. Whisk the sugar and eggs until light and fluffy.
3 Sift the flour and ground almonds on to the egg mixture. Using a large metal spoon, fold gently, then add the orange purée and melted butter. Fold in gently until just mixed. Pour the cake mixture into the prepared tin. Bake for 40–45 minutes until the cake is brown and springs back when lightly pressed. Cool in the tin for 5 minutes. Mix the icing sugar and juice together, drizzle, and serve with crème fraîche.

• Per serving (for eight) 307 kcalories, protein 6g, carbohydrate 41g, fat 14g, saturated fat 4g, fibre 2g, added sugar 30g, salt 0.29g .

Made with ground almonds and dark chocolate, this flourless cake is beautifully dark, rich and moist.

Seriously Rich Chocolate Cake

100g/4oz butter, diced
140g/5oz best-quality dark chocolate, broken into pieces
6 eggs, separated
140g/5oz ground almonds
1 tbsp kirsch or Cointreau (optional)
85g/3oz caster sugar
cocoa powder, for dusting
crème fraîche, to serve

Takes 55 minutes • Serves 8–10

1 Preheat the oven to 170°C/Gas 3/fan oven 150°C. Butter and line the base of a 23cm/9in springform cake tin. Dust the sides with a little flour. Melt the butter and chocolate, stir until smooth, and leave for about 5 minutes to cool slightly. Stir in the egg yolks, ground almonds, and the liqueur, if using.
2 Put the egg whites into a bowl, add a pinch of salt and whisk until soft peaks form. Continue whisking, sprinkling in the sugar a little at a time, until stiff peaks form. Stir 2 tablespoons of the whites into the chocolate mixture, then carefully fold in the remainder.
3 Spoon the mixture into the prepared tin and bake for 30–35 minutes until well risen and just firm. Cool in the tin. Remove the cake and peel away the paper. Dust with cocoa powder, slice, and serve with crème fraîche.

• Per serving (for eight) 401 kcalories, protein 10g, carbohydrate 24g, fat 30g, saturated fat 11g, fibre 2g, added sugar 22g, salt 0.66g

Chocolate and orange is a classic combination.

Dark Chocolate and Orange Cake

1 Seville orange
3 eggs
280g/10oz caster sugar
240ml/8½fl oz sunflower oil
100g/4oz dark chocolate, broken
into pieces and melted
25g/1oz cocoa powder
250g/9oz plain flour
1½ tsp baking powder

FOR THE CHOCOLATE GANACHE
200g/8oz dark chocolate, broken
into pieces
225ml/8fl oz double cream
candied orange zest, to decorate

Takes 2 hours 10 minutes,
plus 1½ hours cooling time •
Serves 10

1 Pierce the orange with a skewer. Cook in a pan of boiling water for 30 minutes. Remove and whizz the whole orange in a food processor. Discard any pips and cool.
2 Preheat the oven to 180°C/Gas 4/fan oven 160°C. Butter and line the base of a 23cm/9in round cake tin. Lightly beat the eggs, sugar and oil. Gradually beat in the puréed orange and cooled, melted chocolate. Sift in the cocoa, flour and baking powder. Mix well and pour into the tin. Bake for 55–60 minutes. Cool for 10 minutes, then turn out on to a wire rack.
3 Put the ganache chocolate into a heatproof bowl. Boil the cream in a pan, pour over the chocolate, and stir until smooth. Cool, up to 1½ hours, until firm. Spread over the cake, and decorate with the candied zest.

• Per serving 703 kcalories, protein 7g, carbohydrate 73g, fat 45g, saturated fat 16g, fibre 2g, added sugar 51g, salt 0.42g

Moist and fruity enough to serve warm with cream for pud, but just as good cold.

Pear, Hazelnut and Chocolate Cake

100g/4oz blanched hazelnuts
140g/5oz self-raising flour
175g/6oz butter, cut into small pieces
140g/5oz golden caster sugar
2 large eggs, beaten
5 small ripe Conference pears
50g/2oz dark chocolate, chopped into small chunks
2 tbsp apricot jam

Takes 1½ hours • Serves 8

1 Preheat the oven to 160°C/Gas 3/fan oven 140°C. Butter and line the base of a 20cm/8in round cake tin. Grind the hazelnuts in a food processor until fairly fine. Add the flour and mix briefly. Add the butter and pulse until it forms crumbs. Add the sugar and eggs and mix briefly. Peel, core and chop two of the pears. Stir the pears and chocolate lightly into the cake mixture.
2 Spoon the mixture into the prepared tin and smooth the top. Peel, core and slice the remaining pears and scatter over the top of the cake. Press down lightly and bake for 50–60 minutes, until firm to the touch. Cool in the tin for 10 minutes, then turn out and cool on a wire rack. Warm the jam and brush over the top. Serve warm or cold.

• Per serving 470 kcalories, protein 6g, carbohydrate 47g, fat 30g, saturated fat 14g, fibre 3g, added sugar 18g, salt 0.5g

Rich with brandy-steeped prunes, this is a cake
for real lovers of chocolate.

Prune and Chocolate Torte

250g/9oz no-soak prunes, halved
4 tbsp brandy
25g/1oz cocoa powder
100g/4oz dark chocolate (at least
70% cocoa solids), broken into
pieces
50g/2oz butter
175g/6oz golden caster sugar
4 large egg whites
85g/3oz plain flour
1 tsp ground cinnamon
lightly whipped cream, or crème
fraîche, to serve

Takes 1 hour 5 minutes,
plus 30 minutes soaking time •
Serves 8

1 Soak the prunes in brandy for about
30 minutes. Preheat the oven to 190ºC/
Gas 5/fan oven 170ºC. Butter a 23cm/9in
loose-bottomed cake tin. Put the cocoa,
chocolate, butter and 140g/5oz of the sugar
in a pan, add 100ml/3½fl oz hot water and
gently heat until smooth. Leave to cool slightly.
2 Whisk the egg whites to soft peaks, then
gradually whisk in the remaining sugar. Sift
the flour and cinnamon over and gently fold
in with a metal spoon, until almost combined.
Add the chocolate mixture and fold in until
evenly combined.
3 Pour the mixture into the tin and arrange
the prunes over the top. Sprinkle over any
remaining brandy and bake for about
30 minutes until just firm. Serve with cream
or crème fraîche.

• Per serving 311 kcalories, protein 5g, carbohydrate
51g, fat 10g, saturated fat 6g, fibre 3g, added sugar
31g, salt 0.18g

A special treat for dessert or at teatime.

Almond and Chocolate Torte with Apricot Cream

5 egg whites
200g/8oz golden caster sugar
100g/4oz ground almonds
50g/2oz toasted flaked almonds
50g/2oz dark chocolate, chopped

FOR THE APRICOT CREAM
425ml/¾ pint double cream
300g/12oz apricot compote

FOR THE DECORATION
3 tbsp toasted flaked almonds
25g/1oz dark chocolate, shaved
icing sugar, for dusting

Takes 1 hour 5 minutes • Serves 8–12

1 Preheat the oven to 180°C/Gas 4/fan oven 160°C. Butter and line the base of a deep 25cm/10in cake tin. Whisk the egg whites until stiff, then gradually whisk in the golden caster sugar, a tablespoonful at a time.
2 Lightly fold in the ground almonds, the toasted flaked almonds and the chopped chocolate. Pour the mixture into the cake tin and bake for 40–45 minutes until crisp on top and light golden. Allow to cool in the tin for 5 minutes, then turn out and leave to cool on a wire rack.
3 Whip the cream until it just holds its shape. Spoon in the apricot compote, then fold it in gently to give you swirls of apricot. Spoon over the torte and scatter with toasted flaked almonds and chocolate shavings. Dust lightly with sifted icing sugar.

• Per serving (for eight) 574 kcalories, protein 9g, carbohydrate 44g, fat 42g, saturated fat 18g, fibre 3g, added sugar 37g, salt 0.16g

Scatter over a handful of little chocolate eggs for an Easter treat.

Chocca Mocca Caramel Cake

2 tsp instant coffee granules/powder
2 tbsp cocoa
175g/6oz butter, softened
175g/6oz golden caster sugar
2 eggs
2 tbsp golden syrup
200g/8oz self-raising flour
4 tbsp milk
2 × 50g chocolate caramel bars,
broken into pieces

FOR THE ICING
2 × 50g chocolate caramel bars,
broken into pieces
50g/2oz butter
2 tbsp milk
100g/4oz icing sugar, sifted

Takes 1½ hours • Serves 10–12

1 Preheat the oven to 180°C/Gas 4/fan oven 160°C. Butter and line the base of a 20cm/8in round cake tin. Mix the coffee, cocoa and 2 tablespoons hot water to a smooth paste. Put the butter, sugar, eggs, syrup, flour, milk and cocoa paste in a bowl and beat for 2–3 minutes until smooth. Stir the caramel bar pieces into the mixture.
2 Turn the mixture into the prepared tin and smooth. Bake for 50–60 minutes, until the top springs back when you press it lightly. Cool in the tin for 5 minutes, then turn out, peel off the lining paper and leave to cool.
3 For the icing, gently heat the caramel bar pieces, butter and milk until smooth, stirring all the time, then remove from the heat and stir in the icing sugar. Leave to cool. Spread the icing over the top of the cooled cake.

• Per serving (for ten) 474 kcalories, protein 5g, carbohydrate 59g, fat 26g, saturated fat 15g, fibre 1g, added sugar 43g, salt 0.8g

These moist little squares are deliciously chocolatey
without being sickly.

Chocolate Cinnamon Crumb Squares

FOR THE CRUMBLE TOPPING
50g/2oz plain flour
1 tbsp cocoa powder
2 tsp ground cinnamon
50g/2oz light muscovado sugar
50g/2oz butter, cut into pieces

FOR THE CAKE
200g/8oz dark chocolate, broken into pieces
175/6oz butter, softened
200g/8oz light muscovado sugar
3 eggs
175g/6oz self-raising flour
icing sugar, for dusting

Takes 2 hours • Makes 16

1 Preheat the oven to 170ºC/Gas 3/fan oven 150ºC. Butter and line the base and sides of a 20cm/8in square cake tin. For the topping, put the flour, cocoa, cinnamon, sugar and the butter into a food processor, then pulse until the mixture forms a crumble. Set aside.
2 For the cake, put the chocolate in a bowl and melt in the microwave on Medium for 2–3 minutes. Put the butter, sugar, eggs and flour in a bowl and beat for 2–3 minutes, until well mixed. Stir in the chocolate until it is evenly mixed in.
3 Tip the mixture into the tin and smooth. Sprinkle the crumble evenly over the top. Bake for 50–60 minutes, until a skewer inserted comes out clean. Leave to cool for 10 minutes in the tin, then turn out to cool on a wire rack. Dust the top lightly with icing sugar.

• Per square 298 kcalories, protein 3g, carbohydrate 36g, fat 16g, saturated fat 10g, fibre 1g, added sugar 25g, salt 0.43g

This flapjack, bulging with chunks of chocolate
and nuts, is brilliant for lunchboxes.

Chunky Chocolate Nut Flapjacks

200g/8oz oats
25g/1oz desiccated coconut
140g/5oz butter, cut into pieces
50g/2oz light muscovado sugar
5 tbsp golden syrup
100g/4oz brazil nuts (or cashews),
cut into large chunks
50g/2oz almonds, cut into large
chunks
85g/3oz good-quality dark
chocolate, broken into
large pieces

Takes 45 minutes • Makes 12

1 Preheat the oven to 180°C/Gas 4/fan
oven 160°C. Lightly butter a 23cm/9in
square tin and line the base. Mix together
the oats and coconut.
2 Put the butter, sugar and syrup in a pan,
cook over a low heat, stirring occasionally,
until the butter has melted and the sugar
dissolved. Remove from the heat and stir in
the oat and coconut mixture. Spoon into the
tin and press down evenly. Scatter over the
nuts and press lightly into the mixture. Stick
the chunks of chocolate between the nuts.
Bake for 25–30 minutes, or until a pale
golden colour.
3 Mark into bars or squares with the back
of a knife while still warm, then allow to cool
completely before cutting through and
removing from the tin.

• Per flapjack 325 kcalories, protein 5g, carbohydrate
28g, fat 22g, saturated fat 10g, fibre 2g, added sugar
15g, salt 0.3g

Deliciously moist, chocolatey and utterly irresistible – they'll keep for up to a week, tightly wrapped in foil.

Banana Nut Brownies

175g/6oz butter, cut into pieces
300g/10oz light muscovado sugar
175g/6oz dark chocolate, broken into pieces
100g bag nuts, toasted and chopped
3 eggs, beaten
2 ripe bananas, mashed
100g/4oz self-raising flour
2 tbsp cocoa powder
1 tsp baking powder

Takes 50 minutes • Makes 15

1 Preheat the oven to 180°C/Gas 4/fan oven 160°C. Butter and line an 18 × 28cm/7 × 11in Swiss roll tin with baking paper. Put the butter, sugar and chocolate in a large pan and heat gently, stirring, until melted and smooth, then remove the pan from the heat.
2 Stir in the nuts, eggs and bananas until well mixed, then sift in the flour, cocoa and baking powder.
3 Pour the mixture into the tin and bake for 30 minutes until firm in the centre. Cool in the tin, then turn out and cut into 15 squares.

• Per brownie 336 kcalories, protein 5g, carbohydrate 37g, fat 20g, saturated fat 9g, fibre 1g, added sugar 28g, salt 0.5g

This no-bake treat is great for lunchboxes.

Choc Crunchies

200g/8oz digestive biscuits
100g/4oz butter
3 tbsp golden syrup
2 tbsp cocoa powder
50g/2oz raisins
100g/4oz dark chocolate

Takes 50 minutes • Serves 8–10

1 Butter an 18cm/7in sandwich tin. Seal the biscuits in a strong polythene bag and bash into uneven crumbs with a rolling pin.
2 Melt the butter and syrup in a pan (or microwave on High for about 1½ minutes). Stir in the cocoa and raisins, then thoroughly stir in the biscuit crumbs. Spoon into the tin and press down firmly.
3 Melt the chocolate in a heatproof bowl over a pan of simmering water (or microwave on Medium for 2–3 minutes). Spread over the biscuit base and chill for about half an hour. Keeps for up to 1 week wrapped in foil.

• Per serving (for eight) 327 kcalories, protein 3g, carbohydrate 36g, fat 20g, saturated fat 11g, fibre 1g, added sugar 17g, salt 0.77g

These little squares are a tempting combination of chewy marshmallows and crunchy nuts, coated with chocolate.

Rocky Road Squares

500g/18oz milk or dark chocolate, broken into pieces
10 marshmallows, cut into small pieces
85g/3oz pecans, almonds or walnuts (or a mixture), roughly chopped

Takes 15 minutes, plus 2 hours cooling • Makes 50

1 Line a shallow 20cm/8in square cake tin with baking paper. In a heatproof bowl set over a pan of simmering water, gently melt the chocolate, then stir in the marshmallows and nuts, mixing well.

2 Pour the mixture into the tin and smooth the top. Leave to set for about 2 hours. Dip a sharp knife in hot water and wipe; cut the cooled mixture into 2.5cm/1in squares.

• Per square 67 kcalories, protein 1g, carbohydrate 7g, fat 4g, saturated fat 2g, fibre trace, added sugar 5g, salt 0.02g

These moreish bars can be frozen, unfrosted,
for up to 2 months.

Cappuccino Bars

1 tsp cocoa powder, plus extra
for dusting
2 rounded tbsp coffee granules
225g/8oz butter, softened
225g/8oz caster sugar
4 eggs
225g/8oz self-raising flour
1 tsp baking powder

FOR THE WHITE CHOCOLATE
FROSTING
100g/4oz white chocolate, broken
into pieces
50g/2oz butter, softened
3 tbsp milk
175g/6oz icing sugar

Takes 50 minutes • Makes 24

1 Preheat the oven to 180°C/Gas 4/fan
oven 160°C. Butter and line the bottom of
a shallow 28 × 18cm/11 × 7in oblong tin.
Mix the cocoa and coffee granules into
2 tablespoons warm water. Put in a large
bowl with the other cake ingredients.
2 Whisk for about 2 minutes with an electric
hand blender to combine, then tip into the
tin and level out. Bake for 35–40 minutes
until risen and firm to the touch. Cool in the
tin for 10 minutes, then cool on a rack. Peel
off the paper.
3 For the frosting, melt the chocolate, butter
and milk in a bowl over a pan of simmering
water. Remove the bowl and sift in the icing
sugar. Beat until smooth, then spread over the
cake. Finish with a dusting of cocoa powder.
Cut into 24 bars.

• Per bar 219 kcalories, protein 3g, carbohydrate 27g,
fat 12g, saturated fat 6g, fibre trace, added sugar 19g,
salt 0.43g

Unrefined dark muscovado sugar gives these brownies
a sticky toffee flavour.

Toffee Brownies

350g/12oz dark chocolate
(preferably around 50–60% cocoa
solids), broken into pieces
250g/9oz unsalted butter, cut
into pieces
3 large eggs
250g/9oz dark muscovado sugar
85g/3oz plain flour
1 tsp baking powder

Takes 1 hour 5 minutes, plus 1 hour
cooling • Makes 16

1 Preheat the oven to 160°C/Gas 3/fan oven 140°C. Butter and line the base of a shallow 23cm/9in square cake tin. Melt the chocolate and butter together, then stir well and cool.
2 Whisk the eggs until pale, then whisk in the sugar until thick and glossy and well combined. Gently fold in the melted chocolate mixture, then sift in the flour and baking powder and gently stir until smooth.
3 Pour into the prepared cake tin and bake for 30–35 minutes, or until firm to the touch. Test by inserting a wooden cocktail stick into the middle – there should be a few moist crumbs sticking to it. The mixture will still be soft in the centre, but will firm up on cooling.
4 Cool in the tin on a wire rack for at least 1 hour, then cut into 16 squares and finish cooling on the rack.

• Per brownie 324 kcalories, protein 3g, carbohydrate 34g, fat 20g, saturated fat 12g, fibre 1g, added sugar 30g, salt 0.14g

A treat for tea by the fire, this afternoon bake keeps moist, well-wrapped, for 4–5 days.

Mincemeat and Marzipan Teabread

200g/8oz self-raising flour
100g/4oz cold butter, cut into pieces
85g/3oz light muscovado sugar
85g/3oz marzipan, cut into 1cm/½in cubes
2 eggs
300g/10oz mincemeat
2 tbsp flaked almonds
icing sugar, for dusting (optional)

Takes 1 hour 20 minutes • Serves 12

1 Preheat the oven to 180ºC/Gas 4/fan oven 160ºC. Butter a 1kg/2lb loaf tin and line the base with greaseproof paper. Tip the flour into a bowl, add the cold butter and rub until the mixture forms fine crumbs. Stir in the sugar and marzipan cubes.
2 In another bowl, lightly whisk the eggs, then stir in the mincemeat. Stir this into the flour mixture until evenly combined. Spoon into the prepared loaf tin, smooth, and sprinkle the flaked almonds over the top. Bake for 1 hour until the teabread is risen and golden brown, or a skewer inserted comes out clean. Lightly dust the teabread with icing sugar while it is still hot.
3 Allow to cool in the tin for 10 minutes, then tip on to a wire rack to cool completely. Peel off the lining paper and cut into slices – it's also very good spread with butter.

• Per serving 265 kcalories, protein 4g, carbohydrate 41g, fat 11g, saturated fat 5g, fibre 1g, added sugar 15g, salt 0.44g

The natural sweetness provided by the bananas helps
reduce the amount of sugar that needs to be used.

Banana Teabread

175g/6oz plain wholemeal flour
50g/2oz medium oatmeal
100g/4oz butter, softened
100g/4oz dark muscovado sugar
2 tsp baking powder
¼ tsp ground cinnamon
2 eggs, beaten
3–4 ripe bananas, about 350g/12oz,
peeled and mashed
100g/4oz walnuts, roughly chopped

Takes 1 hour 35 minutes • Serves 10

1 Preheat the oven to 180°C/Gas 4/fan
oven 160°C. Butter and line the base of
a 1kg/2lb loaf tin with baking paper. Put the
wholemeal flour, oatmeal, butter, sugar,
baking powder, cinnamon and eggs into a
large bowl and, using an electric hand
whisk, beat together until evenly mixed. Stir
in the bananas and walnuts, taking care
not to overmix.
2 Spoon the mixture into the prepared tin
and bake for 1¼ hours or until a skewer
inserted comes out clean (cover the cake
with foil halfway through cooking to prevent
the top from overbrowning). Allow the cake
to cool in the tin for 5 minutes, then carefully
turn out, peel off the lining paper and cool
completely on a wire rack.

• Per serving 309 kcalories, protein 6g, carbohydrate
34g, fat 17g, saturated fat 3g, fibre 3g, added sugar
10g, salt 0.53g

Choose a richly flavoured Greek or Mexican honey
for an extra-special taste.

Walnut, Date and Honey Cake

225g/8oz self-raising flour
½ tsp ground cinnamon
175g/6oz butter, softened
100g/4oz light muscovado sugar
3 tbsp clear honey
2 eggs, beaten
2 medium, ripe bananas, about
250g/9oz total weight
in their skins
100g/4oz stoned dates
50g pack walnut pieces

Takes 1 hour 25 minutes •
Serves 8–10

1 Preheat the oven to 160°C/Gas 3/fan oven 140°C. Line the base and long sides of a 1kg/2lb loaf tin with greaseproof paper, buttering the tin and paper. Tip the flour, cinnamon, butter, sugar, 2 tablespoons of the honey and the eggs into a large mixing bowl. Mash the bananas and chop the dates (kitchen scissors are easiest for this), and add to the bowl. Beat the mixture for 2–3 minutes, using a wooden spoon or hand-held mixer, until well blended.

2 Spoon into the prepared tin and smooth. Scatter the walnut pieces over the top. Bake for 1 hour, then lightly press the top – it should feel firm. If not, bake for a further 10 minutes.

3 Cool for 15 minutes, then lift out of the tin using the paper. When cold, drizzle the remaining honey over. Cut into thick slices.

• Per serving (for eight) 440 kcalories, protein 6g, carbohydrate 54g, fat 24g, saturated fat 13g, fibre 1.5g, added sugar 25g, salt 0.7g

Measuring the ingredients in a jug makes this really easy to throw together – though it does need to be started the day before baking.

Peach and Cherry Teabread

300ml/½ pint ready-to-eat dried peaches, chopped
150ml/¼ pint undyed glacé cherries, halved
150ml/¼ pint raisins
300ml/½ pint light muscovado sugar
300ml/½ pint freshly made hot tea
1 egg, beaten
1 pint self-raising flour
1 tsp ground cinnamon
icing sugar, for dusting

Takes 1¾ hours, plus overnight soaking • Serves 12–14

1 Put the fruit and sugar in a bowl, pour over the tea and stir well. Cover with a tea towel and leave overnight for the fruit to plump up.

2 Preheat the oven to 160°C/Gas 3/fan oven 140°C. Butter and line the base of a 1kg/2lb loaf tin with greaseproof paper. Stir the egg into the steeped fruit mixture, then sift in the flour and cinnamon. Mix well, then turn into the prepared tin and smooth the top.

3 Bake for 1¼–1½ hours until the teabread is risen and golden. Test with a skewer (it should come out clean). Cool in the tin for 10 minutes, then turn out and cool on a wire rack. Dust the top with icing sugar.

• Per serving (for twelve) 297 kcalories, protein 4g, carbohydrate 71g, fat 1g, saturated fat 0.4g, fibre 3g, added sugar 31g, salt 0.31g

Made in a flash, this is best cut into thick slices
and spread with butter while still warm.

Spotted Dog

300g/10oz plain flour
½ tsp salt
1 tsp bicarbonate of soda
3 tbsp caster sugar
100g/4oz mixed dried fruit
1 egg, beaten
200ml/7fl oz buttermilk

Takes 50 minutes • Serves 10–12

1 Preheat the oven to 190°C/Gas 5/fan oven 170°C. Butter a 1kg/2lb loaf tin. Sift the flour, salt and bicarbonate of soda into a mixing bowl. Stir in the sugar, make a well in the centre and add the dried fruit, egg and buttermilk. Mix lightly and quickly into the flour for a soft dough.
2 Using floured hands, remove the dough from the bowl and knead very briefly. Then press the dough into the prepared tin. Bake for 35–40 minutes until the top is a dark golden colour and the loaf feels firm to the touch. Turn out and leave to cool. Serve thickly sliced and buttered.

• Per serving (for ten) 163 kcalories, protein 4g, carbohydrate 36g, fat 1g, saturated fat 0.3g, fibre 1g, added sugar 5g, salt 0.66g

Use a chunky marmalade to give this loaf extra
texture and a pretty top.

Sticky Marmalade Tealoaf

140g/5oz marmalade (about
one third of a 454g jar)
175g/6oz butter, softened
175g/6oz light muscovado sugar
3 eggs, beaten
225g/8oz self-raising flour
½ tsp baking powder
2 tsp ground ginger
1 tsp mixed spice
100g packet pecan halves

Takes 1½ hours • Serves 12

1 Preheat the oven to 180°C/Gas 4/fan oven
160°C. Butter a 1kg/2lb loaf tin and line with
greaseproof paper. Set aside 1 tablespoon of
the marmalade in a small pan. In a bowl,
blend the remaining marmalade, butter, sugar,
eggs, flour, baking powder and spices for
1–2 minutes until smooth and light. Stir in
about three quarters of the pecans.
2 Tip into the prepared tin and smooth the
top. Sprinkle with the reserved pecans. Bake
for about 1–1¼ hours until a skewer inserted
comes out clean. Cover loosely with foil after
40 minutes. Once cooked, carefully remove
from the tin, and cool slightly on a wire rack.
3 Gently heat the reserved marmalade,
stirring until it's smooth, and spread the glaze
over the top of the warm loaf. Serve in slices.

• Per serving 339 kcalories, protein 4g, carbohydrate
40g, fat 20g, saturated fat 8g, fibre 1g, added sugar
24g, salt 0.56g

Moist and moreish, this rich cake has the most
wonderful, crunchy sugarplum topping.

Autumn Plum Crunch Cake

2 eggs, plus 1 egg yolk
140g/5oz butter, softened
140g/5oz golden caster sugar
140g/5oz self-raising flour
grated zest and juice of 1 orange
200g/8oz plums, stoned, half
roughly chopped into pieces
and half cut into wedges

FOR THE TOPPING
1½ tbsp fresh lemon juice
200g/8oz golden caster sugar
25g/1oz rough sugar pieces
(or sugar cubes), roughly
crushed

Takes 1½ hours • Serves 10

1 Preheat the oven to 160°C/Gas 3/fan
oven 140°C. Butter and line the base of
a 1kg/2lb loaf tin. Lightly beat the eggs
and egg yolk with a pinch of salt.
2 Beat the butter and sugar in a bowl until
light and fluffy. Pour in the eggs a little at a
time, beating well after each addition. Fold
in the flour with the orange zest and two
tablespoons of the juice, then fold in the
roughly chopped plums. Spoon into the
prepared tin and scatter the plum wedges
over. Bake for 50 minutes or until a skewer
inserted comes out clean.
3 Cool for 10 minutes, then turn out on a
wire rack. Mix the remaining orange juice with
the lemon juice and caster sugar. Spoon over
the cooling cake and sprinkle with the
crushed sugar pieces. Cool until set.

• Per serving 327 kcalories, protein 3g, carbohydrate
51g, fat 14g, saturated fat 8g, fibre 1g, added sugar
38g, salt 0.45g

Although a fast and easy recipe for tea,
this loaf is best made a day or two in advance.

Date and Walnut Tea Loaf

200g/8oz stoned dates, chopped
1 tsp bicarbonate of soda
100g/4oz butter, cut into pieces
280g/10oz self-raising flour, sifted
50g/2oz chopped walnuts
100g/4oz dark muscovado sugar
1 egg, beaten
2 tbsp demerara sugar

Takes 1 hour 40 minutes, plus cooling
time • Serves 10–12

1 Mix the dates and bicarbonate of soda in a large bowl with a pinch of salt. Pour in 300ml/½ pint hot water, stir well and leave until cold. Preheat the oven to 180°C/Gas 4/ fan oven 160°C. Butter a 1kg/2lb loaf tin and line the base and two long sides.
2 Rub the butter pieces into the flour until the mixture resembles coarse breadcrumbs. Stir in the walnuts and muscovado sugar until evenly combined.
3 Tip the flour mixture and the egg into the cooled dates. Beat well to mix, then pour into the prepared tin and sprinkle the demerara sugar on top. Bake in the oven for 1–1¼ hours or until a skewer come out clean. Cool in the tin for 5 minutes, then turn it out on to a wire rack. Double-wrap the cooled cake, and store in an airtight tin for 1–2 days before eating.

• Per serving (for ten) 317 kcalories, protein 5g, carbohydrate 49g, fat 13g, saturated fat 6g, fibre 2g, added sugar 14g, salt 0.9g

*The pumpkin adds a depth of flavour, a certain sweetness
and a lusciously moist texture.*

Pumpkin and Ginger Teabread

175g/6oz butter, melted
140g/5oz clear honey
1 large egg, beaten
250g/9oz raw peeled pumpkin or
butternut squash, coarsely
grated (about 500g/1lb 2oz
before peeling and seeding)
100g/4oz light muscovado sugar
350g/12oz self-raising flour
1 tbsp ground ginger
2 tbsp demerara sugar, plus extra
for sprinkling (optional)

Takes 1½ hours • Serves 10

1 Preheat the oven to 180ºC/Gas 4/fan oven 160ºC. Butter and line the base and two long sides of a 1kg/2lb loaf tin with a strip of baking paper.
2 Mix the butter, honey and egg and stir in the pumpkin or squash. Then mix in the sugar, flour and ginger.
3 Pour into the prepared tin and sprinkle the top with the 2 tablespoons of demerara sugar. Bake for 50–60 minutes, until risen and golden brown. Leave in the tin for 5 minutes, then turn out and cool on a wire rack. Sprinkle more demerara sugar over the warm cake, if you wish. Serve thickly sliced and buttered.

• Per serving 351 kcalories, protein 4g, carbohydrate 52g, fat 15g, saturated fat 9g, fibre 1g, added sugar 24g, salt 0.69g

Try other fruits when in season – raspberries
and tayberries would be good.

Blackberry and Apple Loaf

250g/9oz self-raising flour
175g/6oz butter
175g/6oz light muscovado sugar
½ tsp cinnamon
2 rounded tbsp demerara sugar
1 small eating apple, unpeeled,
coarsely grated down to the core
2 large eggs, beaten
finely grated zest of 1 orange
1 tsp baking powder
225g/8oz blackberries

Takes 2 hours • Serves 10

1 Preheat the oven to 180°C/Gas 4/fan oven 160°C. Butter and line the base of a 1kg/2lb loaf tin. Rub the flour, butter and muscovado sugar together to make fine crumbs. Reserve 5 tablespoons of this mixture for the topping, and mix into it the cinnamon and demerara sugar. Set aside.
2 Mix the apple in with the eggs and the zest. Stir the baking powder into the rubbed-in mixture, then quickly and lightly stir in the egg mixture. Don't overmix.
3 Gently fold in three quarters of the berries. Spoon into the tin and level. Scatter the rest of the berries on top. Sprinkle over the topping and bake for 1 hour 20 minutes, testing with a skewer. After 50 minutes, cover loosely with foil. Leave in the tin for 30 minutes, then cool on a wire rack.

• Per serving 327 kcalories, protein 4g, carbohydrate 44g, fat 16g, saturated fat 10g, fibre 2g, added sugar 23g, salt 0.77g

Sealed in a plastic food bag, this loaf will freeze
for up to 3 months.

Banana and Walnut Tea Loaf

100g/4oz butter, softened
140g/5oz light muscovado sugar
2 eggs, lightly beaten
100g/4oz walnuts, chopped
2 ripe bananas, mashed
2 tbsp milk
225g/8oz self-raising flour

Takes 1¼ hours • Serves 12

1 Preheat the oven to 180°C/Gas 4/fan oven 160°C. Butter and line a 1kg/2lb loaf tin. Cream the butter and sugar, then add the eggs. Set aside 25g/1oz walnuts, then fold the rest into the creamed mixture with the bananas and milk. Fold in the flour. Spoon into the tin and sprinkle over the reserved walnuts.

2 Bake for 55–60 minutes until risen. Stand for 10 minutes, then turn out, remove the lining paper and cool.

• Per serving 267 kcalories, protein 4g, carbohydrate 33g, fat 14g, saturated fat 5g, fibre 1g, added sugar 12g, salt 0.37g

Unrefined caster sugar and a salted or slightly salted creamy butter will give the best flavour.

Shortbread

150g/6oz plain flour
100g/4oz slightly salted butter, cut into pieces and softened
50g/2oz golden caster sugar
caster sugar, for sprinkling

Takes 50 minutes • Serves 8

1 Preheat the oven to 150°C/Gas 2/fan oven 130°C. Put the flour in a mixing bowl, add the butter and rub together to make fine crumbs. Stir in the sugar.

2 Work the mixture together until it forms a ball. Turn out on to a work surface and knead briefly until smooth. Roll and pat out on a very lightly floured surface to an 18cm/7in round. Smooth the surface with your hands. Carefully slide the dough on to an ungreased baking sheet and flute the edges. Mark the circle into eight triangles with a knife, not cutting all the way through. Prick the surface all over with a fork.

3 Bake for 30–35 minutes or until cooked. The shortbread should be very pale. While still warm, cut through the markings and sprinkle with caster sugar. Cool before eating.

• Per serving 186 kcalories, protein 2g, carbohydrate 22g, fat 10g, saturated fat 7g, fibre 1g, added sugar 8g, salt trace

Buttermilk adds a lightness that milk alone
won't give you.

Buttermilk Scones

350g/12oz self-raising flour
100g/4oz caster sugar
85g/3oz butter, cut into small pieces
about 175ml/6fl oz buttermilk or
natural low-fat yogurt
whipped cream and strawberry jam,
to serve

Takes 25 minutes • Makes 12

1 Preheat the oven to 200°C/Gas 6/fan oven 180°C. Mix together the flour and sugar in a bowl. Rub the butter in with your fingertips until the mixture resembles fine breadcrumbs. Make a well in the centre of the ingredients and tip in the buttermilk, all in one go, then mix lightly to form a soft dough.
2 Tip the dough out on to a lightly floured surface and knead briefly. Press the dough out to a 2.5cm/1in thickness, then stamp out 5cm/2in rounds with a cutter. Gather up the trimmings, knead again briefly and stamp out more rounds.
3 Transfer the buttermilk scones to a baking sheet, spaced a little apart, and bake for 12–15 minutes until risen and light golden. Leave the scones to cool on a wire rack and serve with the whipped cream and jam.

• Per scone 187 kcalories, protein 3g, carbohydrate 32g, fat 6g, saturated fat 4g, fibre 1g, added sugar 9g, salt 0.42g

These light and luscious tarts are a cross between the traditional Yorkshire curd tart and the lemony Portuguese version.

Cinnamon and Lemon Tarts with Berries

375g pack ready-rolled puff pastry
200g pack light soft cheese
grated rind of ½ lemon
100g/4oz caster sugar
2 egg yolks
1 tbsp plain flour

TO SERVE
100g/4oz each of raspberries and blueberries
cinnamon and icing sugar, for dusting
142ml carton single cream (optional)

Takes 45 minutes • Serves 6

1 Preheat the oven to 200°C/Gas 6/fan oven 180°C. Unwrap the pastry, then roll it out so you can stamp out 12 rounds using an 7.5cm/3in fluted cutter. Line 12 bun tins with the pastry and prick them with a fork all over (this is essential to stop the pastry rising up in the centre and tipping the filling out).
2 Beat the cheese until soft, then beat in the lemon rind, sugar and egg yolks. Sift in the flour and mix well. Pour into the pastry cases, almost to the top.
3 Bake the tarts for 12–15 minutes, until the pastry is golden and the filling lightly coloured. Carefully remove from the tins and leave aside on a rack to cool. To serve, place 2 tarts on a plate, scatter the berries over, dust lightly with cinnamon and icing sugar, then drizzle with a little cream, if you like.

• Per serving 411 kcalories, protein 8g, carbohydrate 48g, fat 22g, saturated fat 1g, fibre 1g, added sugar 19g, salt 0.76g

Decorated with ready-made writing icing and tiny sugar flowers, these little cakes couldn't be easier.

Mother's Day Fairy Cakes

FOR THE CAKES
175g/6oz caster sugar
175g/6oz butter, softened
3 eggs, beaten
175g/6oz self-raising flour
1 tsp baking powder

FOR THE DECORATION
140g/5oz icing sugar, sifted
yellow food colouring
a selection of writing icings
(available in supermarkets)
ready-made sugar flowers (sold
with the cake ingredients)
paper cake cases

Takes 30 minutes • Makes 20

1 Preheat the oven to 190ºC/Gas 5/fan oven 170ºC. Put the cake cases into bun tins. In a bowl, mix all the cake ingredients and beat with an electric whisk for about 1–2 minutes, until evenly mixed.
2 Put a heaped tablespoon of the cake mixture into the centre of each paper case. Bake for 15 minutes, or until golden and well risen. Remove the cakes from the oven and cool on a wire rack.
3 Mix the icing sugar with 4 teaspoons of cold water to make a smooth paste, then colour with a drop or two of the yellow food colouring. Spread a teaspoon of the icing on each bun. Leave to set. Using the writing icing, pipe one letter of 'Happy Mother's Day' (or whatever occasion you're celebrating) on to each of the fairy cakes. Leave to set.

• Per fairy cake 186 kcalories, protein 2g, carbohydrate 28g, fat 8g, saturated fat 5g, fibre trace, added sugar 21g, salt 0.46g

Traditional simnel cake can be a bit too rich – instead, try these light little muffins with a gooey nugget of marzipan baked in the centre.

Simnel Muffins

250g/9oz mixed dried fruit
grated zest and juice of 1 medium orange
175g/6oz butter, softened
175g/6oz golden caster sugar
3 eggs, beaten
300g/10oz self-raising flour
1 tsp mixed spice
½ tsp freshly grated nutmeg
5 tbsp milk
175g/6oz marzipan

FOR DECORATING
200g/8oz icing sugar
2 tbsp orange juice for mixing
sugar eggs or mini eggs

Takes 55 minutes • Makes 12

1 Tip the fruit into a bowl, add the zest and juice and microwave on Medium for 2 minutes (or leave to soak for 1 hour). Line 12 deep muffin tins with paper muffin cases. Preheat the oven to 180°C/Gas 4/fan oven 160°C. Beat together the butter, sugar, eggs, flour, spices and milk until light and fluffy, about 3–5 minutes. Stir the fruit in well.
2 Half fill the muffin cases with the mixture. Divide the marzipan into 12 equal pieces, roll into balls, then flatten with your thumb. Put one into each muffin case and spoon the rest of the mixture over. Bake for 25–30 minutes, until risen, golden and firm to the touch.
3 Beat together the icing sugar and orange juice to make icing thick enough to coat the back of a wooden spoon. Drizzle over the cooled muffins and top with a cluster of eggs.

• Per muffin 465 kcalories, protein 6g, carbohydrate 79g, fat 17g, saturated fat 8g, fibre 2g, added sugar 42g, salt 0.61g

This all-in-one cake mixes easily, keeps for a week
wrapped in foil, and freezes well.

Lemon and Violet Drizzle Cake

100g/4oz butter, softened
175g/6oz self-raising flour
1 tsp baking powder
175g/6oz golden caster sugar
2 large eggs
6 tbsp milk
finely grated rind of 1 large lemon

FOR THE ICING AND DECORATION
juice of 1 large lemon (you need
3 tablespoons)
100g/4oz golden caster sugar
crystallized violets and mimosa
balls (or yellow sugar balls), to
decorate

Takes 1 hour • Makes 15

1 Preheat the oven to 180°C/Gas 4/fan oven 160°C. Butter and line the base of a shallow oblong tin (about 18 × 28cm/7 × 11in) with baking paper. Tip all the cake ingredients into a large mixing bowl and beat for 2–3 minutes, until the mixture drops easily off the spoon.

2 Spoon the mixture into the prepared tin and smooth the surface with the back of a spoon. Bake for 30–40 minutes, until golden and firm to the touch. Meanwhile, make the icing: beat together the lemon juice and sugar, pour the mixture evenly over the cake while it is still hot, then leave to cool.

3 Cut the cake into 15 squares. Top each one with a crystallized violet and mimosa ball.

• Per square 175 kcalories, protein 2g, carbohydrate 29g, fat 7g, saturated fat 4g, fibre none, added sugar 19g, salt 0.3g

These light-as-air cakes are sold in every self-respecting coffee shop in Sydney – try them and you too will be hooked.

Blueberry and Lemon Friands

100g/4oz unsalted butter
125g/4½oz icing sugar, plus extra
for dusting
25g/1oz plain flour
85g/3oz ground almonds
3 egg whites
grated rind of 1 unwaxed lemon
85g/3oz blueberries

Takes 40 minutes • Serves 6

1 Preheat the oven to 200°C/Gas 6/fan oven 180°C. Generously butter six non-stick friand or muffin tins. Melt the butter and set aside to cool.

2 Sift the icing sugar and flour into a bowl. Add the almonds and mix everything between your fingers. Whisk the egg whites in another bowl until they form a light, floppy foam. Make a well in the centre of the dry ingredients, tip in the egg whites and lemon rind, then lightly stir in the butter to form a soft batter.

3 Divide the batter among the tins (a large serving spoon is perfect for this job). Sprinkle a handful of blueberries over each cake and bake for 15–20 minutes until just firm to the touch and golden brown. Cool in the tins for 5 minutes, then turn out and cool on a wire rack. To serve, dust lightly with icing sugar.

• Per friand 316 kcalories, protein 5g, carbohydrate 27g, fat 22g, saturated fat 9g, fibre 1g, added sugar 22g, salt 0.09g

These little cakes are easy – fun to make and decorate with the kids.

Blackberry Fairy Cakes

150ml carton low-fat natural yogurt (rinse the pot and use as a measure)
1 pot of caster sugar
1 pot of sunflower oil
2 eggs
2 pots of self-raising flour
250g punnet blackberries, plus extra for decorating
finely grated rind of 1 orange

FOR THE ICING AND DECORATION
1 pot of icing sugar, plus extra for dusting
1 tbsp orange juice
orange food colouring (optional)
50g bar dark chocolate, melted

Takes 35 minutes • Makes 18

1 Preheat the oven to 190ºC/Gas 5/fan oven 180ºC. Line two bun tins with 18 paper cases. Tip the yogurt, sugar, oil and eggs into a bowl and whisk until combined. Tip in the flour, three quarters of the blackberries and half the orange rind; fold into the mixture with a large metal spoon – don't overwork.
2 Fill each bun case three-quarters full with the mixture and bake for 20–25 minutes until the cakes are risen and golden. Turn out and cool on a wire rack.
3 Sift the icing sugar into a bowl, add the remaining orange rind and the orange juice to make a smooth icing. Stir in a few drops of orange food colouring, if you like. Using a teaspoon, spoon a little icing on top of each cooled cake. Decorate with extra blackberries, or drizzled melted chocolate.

• Per fairy cake 177 kcalories, protein 3g, carbohydrate 29g, fat 7g, saturated fat 2g, fibre 1g, added sugar 18g, salt 0.15g

Ideal with a cup of tea at home, or to enjoy
at your next picnic.

Apricot Crumb Squares

FOR THE TOPPING
175g/6oz plain flour
140g/5oz light muscovado sugar
140g/5oz butter, softened
1 tsp ground cinnamon
½ tsp salt

FOR THE CAKE
175g/6oz butter, softened
200g/8oz golden caster sugar
3 large eggs
175g/6oz plain flour
1 tsp baking powder
2–3 tbsp milk
8 fresh apricots (or canned in
natural juice), quartered
icing sugar, for dusting

Takes 1¼ hours • Makes 16

1 Preheat oven to 180°C/Gas 4/fan oven
160°C, and butter a shallow 23cm/9in
square cake tin. Put the five topping
ingredients in a food processor and blend
to make a sticky crumble.
2 In a separate bowl, blend the butter,
sugar, eggs, flour and baking powder using
an electric hand whisk or wooden spoon,
gradually adding enough milk to make a
creamy mixture that drops from a spoon.
Spread in the tin and scatter with apricots.
Top with the crumble and press down.
3 Bake for 45–50 minutes until golden and
a skewer inserted comes out clean. Cool in
the tin, cut into 16 squares and dust with
icing sugar.

• Per square 332 kcalories, protein 4g, carbohydrate
42g, fat 18g, saturated fat 11g, fibre 1g, added sugar
22g, salt 0.52g

These moist but crumbly squares are best eaten on the day,
but will freeze for up to 3 months.

Blackcurrant Crumble Squares

115g/4oz butter, softened
175g/6oz caster sugar
1 egg
280g/10oz self-raising flour
125ml/4fl oz milk
200g/8oz fresh blackcurrants,
destalked

FOR THE CRUMBLE
115g/4oz caster sugar
85g/3oz plain flour
finely grated rind of 1 lemon
50g/2oz butter

Takes 1 hour • Makes 12

1 Preheat the oven to 180°C/Gas 4/fan oven 160°C. Butter a 28 × 18cm/12 × 7in oblong cake tin and line with baking paper. (You could also use a 23cm/9in square tin or a 25cm/10in round tin.)
2 Beat the butter and sugar in a large bowl with an electric hand whisk until the mixture is pale and fluffy. Whisk in the egg, then carefully fold in the flour and milk until thoroughly combined. Spoon into the tin and spread evenly. Sprinkle over the blackcurrants.
3 Mix together the sugar, flour and lemon rind. Rub in the butter until the mixture is crumbly, then sprinkle on top of the squares. Bake for 45 minutes until the topping is golden and the blackcurrants start to burst through; leave to cool in the tin. When cool, lift the cake out, and cut into squares.

• Per square 315 kcalories, protein 4g, carbohydrate 50g, fat 13g, saturated fat 8g, fibre 2g, added sugar 25g, salt 0.29g

Light and chocolatey, these are the perfect
Hallowe'en treat.

Spider Web Chocolate Fudge Muffins

50g/2oz dark chocolate, broken into pieces
85g/3oz butter
1 tbsp milk
200g/8oz self-raising flour
½ tsp bicarbonate of soda
85g/3oz light muscovado sugar
50g/2oz golden caster sugar
1 egg
142ml carton soured cream

FOR THE TOPPING
100g/4oz dark chocolate, broken into pieces and melted
100g/4oz white chocolate, broken into pieces and melted

Takes 50 minutes • Makes 10

1 Preheat the oven to 190°C/Gas 5/fan oven 170°C, and line a muffin tin with 10 paper cases. Heat the chocolate and butter with the milk until melted. Stir and cool.
2 Mix the flour, bicarbonate of soda and both sugars. Beat the egg in another bowl and stir in the soured cream, then pour this on the flour mixture and add the cooled chocolate. Stir just to combine – don't overmix. Spoon into the cases to about three-quarters full. Bake for 20 minutes until well risen. Cool in the tins for a few minutes, then lift out and continue to cool on a wire rack.
3 Spread one muffin with dark chocolate, then pipe four circles of white chocolate on top. Drag a skewer from centre to the edge to create a cobweb effect. Alternate dark chocolate on white for the opposite effect.

• Per mufffin 349 kcalories, protein 5g, carbohydrate 45g, fat 18g, saturated fat 9g, fibre 1g, added sugar 28g, salt 0.59g

Top with marzipan stars or meringue before baking
to vary this festive recipe.

Festive Mince Pies

FOR THE PASTRY
200g/8oz plain flour
50g/2oz ground almonds
140g/5oz butter, chopped into small pieces
grated rind of 1 orange
50g/2oz caster sugar
1 egg yolk

FOR THE FILLING AND DECORATION
200g/8oz mincemeat
1 egg white, lightly whisked
caster sugar, for dusting

Takes 40 minutes, plus 30 minutes chilling time • Makes 18

1 Preheat the oven to 200°C/Gas 6/fan oven 190°C. Whizz the flour, almonds, butter, orange rind and sugar into crumbs. Add the egg yolk and a teaspoon of cold water and pulse until it forms a dough. Wrap in plastic film and chill for 30 minutes.

2 Roll out the dough thinly and stamp out eighteen 7.5cm/3in rounds. Use to line bun tins. Put a heaped teaspoon of mincemeat in each pastry case. Stamp out nine more pastry rounds. Cut out festive shapes from the centre of each round.

3 Cover the pies with the shapes and pastry rounds with the centres removed. Brush the tops with egg white and dust lightly with caster sugar. Bake for 12–15 minutes until the pastry is crisp and golden. Cool in the tins for 5 minutes, then cool on a wire rack.

• Per mince pie 164 kcalories, protein 2g, carbohydrate 20g, fat 9g, saturated fat 5g, fibre 1g, added sugar 9g, salt 0.17g

Absolutely delicious with a cup of tea,
these bars are also dairy free.

Sticky Apricot and Almond Bars

100g/4oz whole blanched almonds
250g/9oz ready-to-eat dried apricots
85g/3oz porridge oats
85g/3oz plain flour
1 tsp baking powder
250ml/9fl oz jar apple sauce
2 tbsp sunflower oil
1 egg, beaten
2 tbsp apricot jam or conserve

Takes 55 minutes • Makes 15

1 Preheat the oven to 180ºC/Gas 4/fan oven 160ºC. Oil and line the base of an 18cm/7in square tin. Roughly chop the almonds into fairly large chunks to give a good texture and finely chop the apricots to give a stickiness to the bars.
2 Put all the dry ingredients in a large bowl. Combine the apple sauce, oil and egg, and add to the dry ingredients. Mix until everything is combined and gooey. Spoon the mixture into the prepared tin, level the surface and bake for 40 minutes or until firm and springy to the touch.
3 Allow to cool in the tin for a couple of minutes, then loosen the sides and turn out on to a wire rack. Warm the apricot jam for 2–3 minutes. Then brush over the surface of the cooled bars, cut into 15 slices and enjoy.

• Per bar 145 kcalories, protein 4g, carbohydrate 19g, fat 6g, saturated fat 1g, fibre 2g, added sugar 3g, salt 0.13g

Margaret Fineran, who created this recipe, was a chef
at the American Embassy in London.

Margaret's Caramel Nut Squares

FOR THE PASTRY
175g/6oz plain flour
50g/2oz icing sugar
85g/3oz cold butter, cut into cubes
¼ tsp vanilla extract
1 small egg, beaten

FOR THE FILLING
85g/3oz granulated sugar
175g/6oz clear honey
50g/2oz butter
284ml carton double cream
100g/4oz pecan nuts, toasted
100g/4oz flaked almonds, toasted
100g/4oz whole hazelnuts, toasted
100g/4oz pistachios, unsalted,
toasted
50g/2oz dried cranberries
whipped cream, to serve

Takes 1¼ hours, plus 4 hours
freezing • Makes 9

1 Preheat the oven to180°C/Gas 4/fan oven 160°C. Whizz together the flour, icing sugar and butter. Add the vanilla and beaten egg and pulse until the pastry comes together. Chill, wrapped in cling film, for 30 minutes.
2 Roll the pastry out on a lightly floured surface and use to line a 23cm/9in square tin. Pre-bake for 7 minutes. Bring the sugar and honey to the boil without stirring. In a separate pan, heat the butter with the cream until hot. When the sugar mixture is boiling, pour in the hot cream and butter, and simmer, stirring, for 2–3 minutes.
3 Mix in the nuts and cranberries. Spoon into the hot pastry case. Return to the oven for 7 minutes. Remove, cool, then cover and freeze for 3–4 hours. Cut into squares, thaw for 30 minutes, and serve with the cream.

• Per square 743 kcalories, protein 10g, carbohydrate 54g, fat 55g, saturated fat 19g, fibre 3g, added sugar 31g, salt 0.35g

The solution for any picnic or open-air event – packed with good things, and easy to make.

Sunshine Bars

100g/4oz dried ready-to-eat tropical medley or other mixed dried fruits
100g/4oz porridge oats
50g/2oz puffed rice cereal, such as Rice Krispies
85g/3oz desiccated coconut
50g/2oz blanched hazelnuts or shelled peanuts or other nuts
50g/2oz sunflower, sesame or pumpkin seeds
100g/4oz light muscovado sugar
125ml/4fl oz golden syrup
100g/4oz butter, cut into pieces

Takes 25 minutes, plus 2 hours setting time • Makes 18

1 Chop the tropical medley into pieces using kitchen scissors. Tip the oats, cereal, coconut and fruit into a large bowl and mix well. Put the hazelnuts and sunflower, sesame or pumpkin seeds in a large frying pan with no oil and, over a moderate heat, stir until they are lightly toasted. Leave to cool a little then tip into the bowl and mix.
2 Put the sugar, syrup and butter in a small pan and heat gently, stirring with a wooden spoon until melted, then simmer for 2 minutes until slightly thicker and syrupy. Quickly stir the syrup into the dry ingredients, mixing until well blended with no dry patches.
3 Quickly tip into a 20cm/8in square tin and press down with the back of a spoon to even out the surface. Leave to cool and set – about 2 hours. Cut the mixture into 18 bars.

• Per bar 190 kcalories, protein 2g, carbohydrate 22g, fat 11g, saturated fat 6g, fibre 2g, added sugar 11g, salt 0.26g

By using different-sized tins and varying the cooking time, this recipe can be adapted to suit all tastes.

Classic Flapjacks

175g/6oz butter, cut into pieces
140g/5oz golden syrup
50g/2oz light muscovado sugar
250g/9oz oats

Takes 35 minutes • Makes 12

1 Preheat the oven to 180°C/Gas 4/fan oven 160°C. Line the base of a shallow 23cm/9in square tin with a sheet of baking paper if the tin is not non-stick. (Use a 20cm/8in square tin for a thicker, chewier flapjack). Put the butter, syrup and sugar in a medium pan. Stir over a low heat until the butter has melted and the sugar has dissolved. Remove from the heat and stir in the oats.

2 Press the mixture into the tin. Bake for 20–25 minutes, until golden brown on top (follow the longer cooking time for a crispier flapjack). Allow to cool in the tin for 5 minutes then mark into bars or squares with the back of a knife while still warm. Cool in the tin completely before cutting and removing – this prevents the flapjack from breaking up.

• Per flapjack 242 kcalories, protein 3g, carbohydrate 29g, fat 14g, saturated fat 8g, fibre 1g, added sugar 13g, salt 0.38g

This easy-mix bar is the perfect bake – all you do is weigh, mix and scatter everything into the tin.

Raspberry and Pine Nut Bars

200g/8oz plain flour
200g/8oz porridge oats
250g pack butter, cut into small pieces and softened
175g/6oz light muscovado sugar
finely grated zest of 1 lemon
100g pack pine nuts
250g/9oz raspberries

Takes 1 hour • Makes 12

1 Preheat the oven to 190°C/Gas 5/fan oven 170°C. Butter a shallow 23cm/9in square tin. Tip the flour, oats and butter into a mixing bowl and work together with your fingers to make coarse crumbs. Mix in the sugar, lemon zest and three quarters of the pine nuts using your hands, then press the mixture together well so it forms large sticky clumps.
2 Drop about two thirds of the oat mixture into the tin, spread it out and press down very lightly – don't pack it too firmly. Scatter the raspberries on top, sprinkle the rest of the oat mixture over, then the rest of the pine nuts and press everything down lightly.
3 Bake for 35–40 minutes until pale golden on top. Cut into 12 bars with a sharp knife while still warm, then leave to cool in the tin before removing.

• Per bar 391 kcalories, protein 6g, carbohydrate 40g, fat 24g, saturated fat 12g, fibre 3g, added sugar 15g, salt 0.41g

These cakes are truly scrumptious and
so simple to whip together.

Starry Toffee Cake Squares

200g/8oz butter
200g/8oz golden syrup
300g/10oz self-raising flour
1 tsp salt
200g/8oz light muscovado sugar
3 eggs
2 tbsp milk
225g/8oz yellow marzipan
red and green food colouring
icing sugar, for dusting

Takes 1½ hours • Makes 24

1 Preheat the oven to 160°C/Gas 3/fan
oven 140°C. Butter and line the base of a
32 × 23 × 2cm/13 × 9 × 1in Swiss roll tin.
Gently melt the butter and syrup in a pan,
stirring to combine. Cool for 15 minutes.
2 Sift the flour with the salt and stir in the
muscovado sugar. Beat in the cooled syrup
mixture. Beat the eggs and milk, and
combine with the flour mixture until smooth.
Pour into the tin and level with a spoon.
Bake for 40–50 minutes until risen and firm
in the centre. Leave in the tin to cool for
10 minutes. Tip on to a wire rack until cold.
3 Divide the marzipan into three; colour one
piece with red and another with green
colouring. Roll out and cut out star shapes.
Cut the cake into 24 squares, top with
marzipan stars and dust with icing sugar.

• Per square 217 kcalories, protein 3g, carbohydrate
34g, fat 9g, saturated fat 5g, fibre 1g, added sugar
22g, salt 0.37g

This is one of those great treats that you can just
sling together and bake.

Golden Orange and Walnut Flapjacks

250g/9oz unsalted butter, chopped
into pieces
250g/9oz golden caster sugar
175g/6oz golden syrup
425g/15oz porridge oats
50g/2oz walnut pieces
finely grated zest of 1 large orange
3 tbsp fine-cut orange marmalade

Takes 55 minutes • Makes 12

1 Preheat the oven to 180ºC/Gas 4/fan oven 160ºC, and generously butter a 28 × 18cm/12 × 7in shallow baking tin. Melt the butter, sugar and syrup over a medium heat, stirring all the time. Take off the heat and stir in the oats, walnuts and orange zest. The mixture should be quite soft.

2 Tip the mixture into the tin and level it off. Bake for around 30 minutes, until the edges are golden brown but the centre is still a little soft. Remove from the oven and mark into 12 pieces while it is still warm, cutting halfway through with a knife. Leave to cool.

3 Heat the marmalade with 1 tablespoon of water until it becomes syrupy. Brush this glaze over the flapjack mixture and leave to cool before cutting into 12 pieces. They will keep in an airtight tin for up to a week.

• Per flapjack 455 kcalories, protein 7g, carbohydrate 60g, fat 22g, saturated fat 12g, fibre 4g, added sugar 36g, salt 0.12g

Combining fruit with fibre is a great energy boost.

Bramley Apple, Fig and Walnut Flapjacks

450g/1lb Bramley apples, peeled and cored
25g/1oz golden caster sugar
grated zest of 1 small lemon
100g/4oz dried ready-to-eat figs, roughly chopped
140g/5oz butter, cut in pieces
50g/2oz light muscovado sugar
140g/5oz golden syrup
250g/9oz porridge oats
½ tsp ground cinnamon
25g/1oz walnuts, finely chopped

Takes 1¼ hours • Makes 9

1 Preheat the oven to 190ºC/Gas 5/fan oven 170ºC. Slice the apples into a small saucepan and stir in the caster sugar. Bring to the boil, cover and simmer for 10 minutes or until the apple is soft, stirring occasionally. Stir in the zest and figs and cook for a further 15 minutes, uncovered, stirring often until the figs are softened and the mixture is quite dry. Whizz to a purée in a food processor.
2 Melt the butter, muscovado sugar and syrup in a saucepan, but don't let it boil. Stir in the oats and cinnamon and mix well.
3 Press half the mixture into an 18cm/7in shallow square sandwich tin. Spread the purée on top and cover with the remaining mixture. Sprinkle over the walnut pieces and bake for 25 minutes or until golden. Remove from the oven, mark into squares and cool.

• Per flapjack 516 kcalories, protein 6g, carbohydrate 66g, fat 27g, saturated fat 14g, fibre 5g, added sugar 24g, salt 0.61g

These are chewier than most flapjacks because of the
bananas mashed in with the oats.

Chewy Gooey Flapjacks

140g/5oz butter
100g/4oz light muscovado sugar
2 heaped tbsp golden syrup
350g/12oz porridge oats (not
jumbo oats)
1 tsp ground cinnamon
½ tsp baking powder
2 medium, ripe bananas

Takes 45 minutes • Makes 18

1 Preheat the oven to 180°C/Gas 4/fan
oven 160°C. Butter a 23 × 33cm/9 × 13in
Swiss roll tin. Melt together the butter, sugar
and syrup in a large saucepan over a low
heat, then stir in the oats, cinnamon, baking
powder and a pinch of salt until well
combined. Peel and mash the bananas and
add to the mixture, stirring well to combine.
Tip into the prepared tin and smooth the
surface with the back of a metal spoon.
2 Bake for 20–25 minutes or until the edges
are just beginning to turn golden brown.
The mixture will feel fairly firm to the touch.
3 Transfer the tin to a wire rack and cut the
mixture into bars while still hot. Leave until
completely cold before removing with a
palette knife.

• Per flapjack 176 kcalories, protein 3g, carbohydrate
25g, fat 8g, saturated fat 4g, fibre 1g, added sugar
8g, salt 0.23g

This bar is deservedly a *Good Food* favourite.

Apple and Apricot Treacle Tart Bars

FOR THE SHORTBREAD BASE
100g/4oz butter, softened
50g/2oz light muscovado sugar
175g/6oz plain flour

FOR THE FRUIT FILLING
450g/1lb (about 2 medium) cooking apples, cored, peeled and chopped
25g/1oz caster sugar
175g/6oz ready-to-eat dried apricots, halved

FOR THE TREACLE TART TOPPING
grated rind of 1 orange, plus 1 tbsp juice
200g/8oz golden syrup
8 tbsp porridge oats

Takes 1½ hours • Makes 12

1 Preheat the oven to 160°C/Gas 3/fan oven 140°C. Beat the butter and sugar until fluffy. Stir in the flour until smooth. Tip the mixture into a 23cm/9in square tin and press down on the base. Lightly prick with a fork and bake for 15 minutes. Set aside to cool.
2 Put the apples in a pan with the sugar. Cover loosely and cook over a low heat, stirring occasionally, for about 10 minutes or until the apples are pulpy. Add the apricots and cook gently, uncovered, for a further 15 minutes, stirring. Whizz to a purée.
3 Increase the oven heat to 190°C/Gas 5/fan oven 170°C. Spread the filling over the base. Combine the topping ingredients until well mixed. Spread over the filling. Return to the oven for a further 20–30 minutes, until set and pale golden. Cool in the tin before cutting.

• Per bar 251 kcalories, protein 3g, carbohydrate 45g, fat 8g, saturated fat 5g, fibre 3g, added sugar 20g, salt 0.29g

Containing marmalade, muesli, orange juice and dried apricots,
these muffins make a wonderful start to your day.

Breakfast Munching Muffins

100g/4oz ready-to-eat dried
apricots, chopped
4 tbsp orange juice
2 large eggs
142ml carton soured cream
100ml/3½fl oz sunflower oil
85g/3oz golden caster sugar
300g/10oz self-raising flour, sifted
1 tsp baking powder
50g/2oz crunchy muesli
12 heaped tsp marmalade

FOR THE TOPPING
50g/2oz light muscovado sugar
2 tbsp sunflower oil
50g/2oz crunchy muesli

Takes 1 hour, plus 20 minutes
soaking • Makes 12

1 Preheat the oven to 190°C/Gas 5/fan oven 170°C. Soak the apricots in the orange juice for 20 minutes or so to plump them up.
2 Beat the eggs in a medium bowl, then mix in the soured cream, oil and sugar. Stir into the apricot mixture. Put the flour, baking powder and muesli in a large bowl, then gently stir in the apricot mixture. Combine thoroughly but quickly – don't overmix or the muffins will be tough.
3 Spoon the mixture into 12 muffin cases (the large paper cases) in a muffin tray. Dip your thumb into a little flour, then make a fairly deep thumbprint in each muffin. Fill each with a heaped teaspoon of marmalade.
4 Combine the topping ingredients and sprinkle over the top of the muffins. Bake for 25–30 minutes, until well risen and golden.

• Per muffin 322 kcalories, protein 5g, carbohydrate 48g, fat 14g, saturated fat 3g, fibre 2g, added sugar 19g, salt 0.51g

These deliciously moist muffins use soya flour, and also contain wholemeal flour and sunflower oil to keep them 'heart friendly'.

Banana and Walnut Muffins

100g/4oz wholemeal flour
25g/1oz soya flour
3 tbsp caster sugar
2 tsp baking powder
85g/3oz walnuts, roughly chopped
1 egg, beaten
50ml/2fl oz sweetened soya milk
50ml/2fl oz sunflower oil
2 large bananas, about 200g/8oz when peeled, roughly chopped

FOR THE DECORATION
3 tbsp apricot jam
50g/2oz chopped walnuts

Takes 40 minutes • Makes 6

1 Preheat the oven to 200ºC/Gas 6/fan oven 180ºC. Line six muffin tins with paper muffin cases or oil the tins. Mix together the first five ingredients in a bowl with a pinch of salt and make a well in the centre.
2 In another bowl, mix together the egg, soya milk and oil. Pour this mixture into the flour and stir until just blended. Gently stir in the bananas. Spoon the mixture into the muffin cases, filling them to about two-thirds full. Bake for 25–30 minutes, until a skewer inserted comes out clean. Transfer the muffins to a wire rack.
3 Gently heat the jam and brush it on top of the muffins. Sprinkle over the walnuts and serve warm.

• Per muffin 425 kcalories, protein 9g, carbohydrate 41g, fat 26g, saturated fat 3g, fibre 3g, added sugar 17g, salt 0.89g

These low-fat muffins are great to grab when you don't
have time to sit down to breakfast.

Fruitburst Muffins

225g/8oz plain flour
2 tsp baking powder
2 large eggs
50g/2oz butter, melted
175ml/6fl oz skimmed milk
100ml/3½fl oz clear honey
140g/5oz fresh blueberries
85g/3oz dried cranberries
140g/5oz seedless raisins
140g/5oz dried apricots, chopped
1 tsp grated orange zest
1 tsp ground cinnamon

Takes 50 minutes • Makes 12

1 Preheat the oven to 200ºC/Gas 6/fan oven 180ºC, and very lightly butter a 12-hole muffin tin. Sift the flour and baking powder into a bowl. In another bowl, lightly beat the eggs, then stir in the melted butter, milk and honey.
2 Add the egg mixture to the flour mixture with the remaining ingredients. Combine quickly without overworking (it's fine if there are some lumps left – you want it gloopy rather than fluid). Spoon the mixture into the muffin tin. Bake for 20–25 minutes until well risen and pale golden on top.
3 Leave in the tin for a few minutes before turning out. When cool, they'll keep in an airtight tin for two days. They can also be frozen for up to one month.

• Per muffin 243 kcalories, protein 5g, carbohydrate 41g, fat 8g, saturated fat 3g, fibre 2g, added sugar 6g, salt 0.59g

Other seasonal berries such as raspberries, loganberries and blueberries also add a delicious fruitiness to these muffins.

Blackberry Muffins

400g/14oz plain flour
175g/6oz caster sugar
1 tbsp baking powder
finely grated zest of 1 orange
½ tsp salt
284ml carton buttermilk
2 eggs, beaten
85g/3oz butter, melted
250g/9oz blackberries

Takes 30 minutes • Makes 12

1 Preheat the oven to 200°C/Gas 6/fan oven 180°C. Butter a 12-hole muffin tin. In a large bowl, combine the flour, sugar, baking powder, zest and salt. In a separate bowl, mix together the buttermilk, eggs and butter.
2 Make a well in the centre of the dry ingredients and pour in the buttermilk mixture. Stir until the ingredients are just combined and the mixture is quite stiff, but be careful not to overmix. Lightly fold in the blackberries, then spoon the mixture into the tins to fill the holes generously.
3 Bake for 15–18 minutes until risen and pale golden on top. Leave to cool in the tin for a few minutes, as the muffins are quite delicate when hot. Run a palette knife around the edge of the muffins and carefully transfer to a wire rack to cool. Best eaten the same day.

• Per muffin 252 kcalories, protein 5g, carbohydrate 44g, fat 7g, saturated fat 4g, fibre 2g, added sugar 15g, salt 0.79g

Each muffin hides a surprise filling of fresh fruit
and creamy cheese.

Strawberry Cheesecake Muffins

350g/12oz plain flour
1½ tbsp baking powder
140g/5oz caster sugar
finely grated rind of 2 medium
oranges
½ tsp salt
2 eggs
250ml/9fl oz milk
85g/3oz butter, melted

FOR THE FILLING
175g/6oz half-fat soft cheese
3 tbsp caster sugar
6 small strawberries, halved

Takes 40 minutes • Makes 12

1 Preheat the oven to 200°C/Gas 6/fan oven 180°C. Line a muffin tin with 12 paper cases. Sift the flour and baking powder into a large bowl, then stir in the sugar, orange rind and salt. Beat the eggs and milk together in a jug or bowl, then stir in the butter and gently mix into the dry ingredients to make a loose, slightly lumpy mixture. Do not overmix or the muffins will be tough.
2 Mix together the soft cheese and sugar for the filling. Half-fill the paper cases with the muffin mixture, then push half a strawberry into each. Top with a teaspoon of sweet cheese, then spoon over the remaining muffin mixture to cover and fill the muffin cases.
3 Bake for 15 minutes until well risen and golden on top. Remove from the tin and allow to cool completely on a wire rack.

• Per muffin 293 kcalories, protein 6g, carbohydrate 42g, fat 12g, saturated fat 5g, fibre 1g, added sugar 18g, salt 1.03g

Banana chips add extra flavour and a crunchy
texture to these muffins.

Banana and Lemon Muffins

85g/3oz honey-dipped dried
banana chips
140g/5oz self-raising flour
2 tsp baking powder
finely grated zest and juice of
1 lemon
4 tbsp light muscovado sugar
5 tbsp milk
1 egg, beaten
50ml/2fl oz sunflower oil
3 bananas
4 tbsp icing sugar

Takes 45 minutes • Makes 7

1 Preheat the oven to 200°C/Gas 6/fan oven
180°C. Lightly oil seven cups of a muffin tin or
line with deep paper cases. Break 50g/2oz of
the banana chips into pieces. Sift together the
flour and baking powder. Stir in the zest,
sugar and the broken dried banana chips.
2 Whisk together the milk, egg and oil. Mash
the bananas with 1 tablespoon of lemon juice.
Fold carefully into the dry ingredients with the
egg mixture (do not overwork it). Divide the
mixture between the muffin cups/cases, not
quite filling them. Bake for 20 minutes until
risen and firm. Leave for a few minutes, then
transfer to a wire rack to cool.
3 Sift the icing sugar into a bowl. Blend
with 1–2 teaspoons of the remaining lemon
juice. Drizzle over the muffins; decorate with
the remaining whole banana chips.

• Per muffin 332 kcalories, protein 4g, carbohydrate
57g, fat 11g, saturated fat 1g, fibre 1g, added sugar
25g, salt 0.76g

If you like the taste of banana loaf, you'll love these moist muffins.

Banana Pecan Muffins

250g/9oz plain flour
25g/1oz natural wheatgerm
1 tsp bicarbonate of soda
1 tsp baking powder
½ tsp ground cinnamon
100g/4oz pecans, roughly chopped
3 small bananas (350g/12oz total
weight in their skins)
1 egg, beaten
85g/3oz butter, melted
100g/4oz light muscovado sugar
175ml/6fl oz buttermilk

Takes 40 minutes • Makes 8

1 Preheat the oven to 200ºC/Gas 6/fan oven 180ºC. Butter 8 holes of a muffin tin. In a large bowl, combine the flour, wheatgerm, bicarbonate, baking powder, cinnamon and 85g/3oz pecans. Peel and mash the bananas.
2 In a separate bowl, mix together the egg, butter and sugar, then stir in the mashed banana and buttermilk. Add the egg mixture all at once to the flour mixture, stirring until just combined, but don't overmix or the result will be heavy.
3 Spoon the mixture into the holes to fill. Sprinkle with the remaining pecans. Bake for 20–25 minutes until well risen and golden. Leave in the tin for 10 minutes, then remove and cool on a wire rack.

• Per muffin 376 kcalories, protein 7g, carbohydrate 47g, fat 19g, saturated fat 6g, fibre 2g, added sugar 13g, salt 0.89g

This mixture will also divide between a 12-hole muffin tin for smaller muffins.

Squash, Cinnamon and Pumpkin Seed Muffins

280g/10oz plain flour
1 tbsp baking powder
2 tsp ground cinnamon
1 tsp salt
3 eggs
175ml/6fl oz milk
85g/3oz butter, melted
175g/6oz light muscovado sugar
350g/12oz peeled, grated butternut squash
small handful of green pumpkin seeds

Takes 50 minutes • Makes 9

1 Preheat the oven to 200°C/Gas 6/fan oven 180°C. Lightly butter a 9-hole muffin tin or line with paper muffin cases. Sift together the flour, baking powder, cinnamon and salt and put aside.

2 In a large bowl, mix the eggs, milk and butter. Add the sugar and beat well. Add the flour mixture and beat to give a lumpy batter. Stir in the grated squash.

3 Fill the nine holes of the muffin tin (or paper cases) to the top with the mixture, sprinkle the pumpkin seeds on top. Bake for 20–25 minutes until well risen and firm to the touch. Cool slightly in the tin, turn out and cool on a wire rack.

• Per muffin 317 kcalories, protein 7g, carbohydrate 50g, fat 12g, saturated fat 6g, fibre 2g, added sugar 20g, salt 1.52g

These muffins have the bonus of lots of health-giving ingredients – so enjoy them without guilt!

Feel-good Muffins

175g/6oz self-raising flour
50g/2oz porridge oats
140g/5oz light muscovado sugar
2 tsp ground cinnamon
½ tsp bicarbonate of soda
1 egg, beaten
150ml/¼ pint buttermilk
1 tsp vanilla extract
6 tbsp sunflower oil
175g/6oz stoned prunes, chopped
85g/3oz pecans

Takes 45 minutes • Makes 6–8

1 Preheat the oven to 200°C/Gas 6/fan oven 180°C. Butter 6–8 muffin tins or line them with muffin cases. Put the flour, oats, sugar, cinnamon and bicarbonate of soda in a large bowl, then rub everything through your fingers, as if making pastry, to ensure the ingredients are evenly blended.
2 In a separate bowl, beat the egg, then stir in the buttermilk, vanilla and oil. Lightly stir the egg mixture into the flour. Fold in the prunes and nuts.
3 Divide between the tins, filling the cases to the brim, then bake for 20–25 minutes until risen and golden. Serve warm or cold.

• Per muffin (for six) 478 kcalories, protein 8g, carbohydrate 66g, fat 22g, saturated fat 2g, fibre 2g, added sugar 24g, salt 0.66g

Although best made with fresh blueberries, you can make these muffins using the same amount of frozen berries.

Berry Buttermilk Muffins

400g/14oz plain flour
175g/6oz caster sugar
1 tbsp baking powder
finely grated rind of 1 lemon
½ tsp salt
284ml carton buttermilk
2 eggs, beaten
85g/3oz butter, melted
250g/9oz fresh or frozen blueberries, or mixed summer fruits, used straight from frozen

Takes 40 minutes • Makes 12

1 Preheat the oven to 200ºC/Gas 6/fan oven 180ºC. Butter a 12-hole muffin tin. In a large bowl, combine the flour, sugar, baking powder, lemon rind and salt. In a separate bowl, mix together the buttermilk, eggs and butter.
2 Make a well in the centre of the dry ingredients and pour in the buttermilk mixture. Stir until the ingredients are just combined and the mixture is quite stiff, but don't overmix. Lightly fold in the berries, then spoon the mixture into the tins to fill generously.
3 Bake for about 25 minutes until risen and pale golden on top. Leave to cool in the tin for about 5 minutes before turning out on to a wire rack, as the muffins are quite delicate when hot.

• Per muffin 253 kcalories, protein 5g, carbohydrate 44g, fat 7g, saturated fat 4g, fibre 1g, added sugar 15g, salt 0.91g

A fluffy light muffin, ideal for lunch alongside big chunks of cheese, or as a snack spread with butter and drizzled with extra honey.

Oat and Honey Muffins

250g/9oz plain flour
85g/3oz porridge oats
1 tbsp baking powder
½ tsp cinnamon
½ tsp salt
85g/3oz raisins
2 eggs, beaten
200ml/7fl oz milk
75ml/2½fl oz vegetable oil
50g/2oz light muscovado sugar
5 tbsp clear honey

Takes 40 minutes • Makes 8

1 Preheat the oven to 200°C/Gas 6/fan oven 180°C. Butter 8 holes of a muffin tin. In a large bowl, combine the flour, oats, baking powder, cinnamon, salt and raisins. In a separate bowl, mix together the eggs, milk, oil, sugar and honey. Stir this into the flour mixture until just combined, but don't overmix – the mixture should be quite runny.
2 Spoon the mixture into the holes to fill. Bake for 20–25 minutes. Leave in the tin for a few minutes. Leave in the tin for a few minutes, then turn out on to a wire rack to cool.

• Per muffin 349 kcalories, protein 7g, carbohydrate 57g, fat 12g, saturated fat 2g, fibre 2g, added sugar 16g, salt 1.18g

Serve these muffins warm, drizzled with a generous
helping of maple syrup.

Cranberry and Poppy Seed Muffins

100g/4oz unsalted butter
284ml carton soured cream
2 large free-range eggs
1 tsp vanilla extract
280g/10oz plain flour
2 tsp baking powder
1 tsp bicarbonate of soda
½ tsp salt
200g/8oz golden caster sugar
4 tsp poppy seeds
140g/5oz fresh or frozen cranberries
(thawed)
maple syrup, to serve

Takes 50 minutes • Makes 10

1 Preheat the oven to 190ºC/Gas 5/fan oven 170ºC. Line 10 muffin tins with large discs of very loosely scrunched and lightly oiled greaseproof paper (they should come up the sides of the tin so they become paper muffin cases). Melt the butter, leave to cool for a minute or two, then beat in the soured cream, followed by the eggs and the vanilla extract.
2 In another bowl, mix the flour, baking powder, bicarbonate of soda, salt, sugar and poppy seeds together. Stir this into the soured cream mixture along with the cranberries.
3 Fill each of the prepared muffin cases generously with the mixture and bake for 20–25 minutes. Test with a skewer – it should pull out clean if muffins are done. Lift on to a cooling rack, spoon over some maple syrup and eat while they are still warm.

• Per muffin 340 kcalories, protein 6g, carbohydrate 45g, fat 16g, saturated fat 9g, fibre 1g, added sugar 21g, salt 0.98g

No chance of keeping these for more than a day – definitely a muffin to eat while still warm and the chocolate is gooey.

Triple Chocolate Chunk Muffins

250g/9oz plain flour
25g/1oz cocoa powder
2 tsp baking powder
½ tsp bicarbonate of soda
85g/3oz each dark and white chocolate, broken into chunks
100g/4oz milk chocolate, broken into chunks
2 eggs, beaten
284ml carton soured cream
85g/3oz light muscovado sugar
85g/3oz butter, melted

Takes 35 minutes • Makes 11

1 Preheat the oven to 200°C/Gas 6/fan oven 180°C. Butter 11 holes of a muffin tin. In a large bowl, combine the flour, cocoa, baking powder, bicarbonate of soda and chocolate. In a separate bowl, mix together the eggs, soured cream, sugar and butter.
2 Add the soured cream mixture to the flour mixture and stir until just combined and the mixture is fairly stiff, but don't overmix. Spoon the mixture into the holes to generously fill.
3 Bake for 20 minutes until well risen. Leave in the tins for about 15 minutes as the mixture is quite tender. Remove from the tins and cool on a wire rack.

• Per muffin 325 kcalories, protein 6g, carbohydrate 37g, fat 18g, saturated fat 11g, fibre 1g, added sugar 17g, salt 0.72g

There are no clever techniques involved with Angela Nilsen's irresistible cookies – just measure, mix, stir and bake.

Angela's All-American Chocolate Chunk Cookies

300g/11oz dark chocolate (about 55% cocoa solids), broken into small chunks
100g bar milk chocolate, broken into small chunks
100g/4oz light muscovado sugar
85g/3oz butter, softened
100g/4oz crunchy peanut butter
1 medium egg
½ tsp vanilla extract
100g/4oz self-raising flour
100g/4oz large salted roasted peanuts

Takes 50 minutes • Makes 12

1 Preheat the oven to 180°C/Gas 4/fan oven 160°C. Melt 100g/4oz of the dark chocolate chunks. Stir, then tip in the sugar, butter, peanut butter, egg and vanilla and beat with a wooden spoon until well mixed. Stir in the flour, all the milk chocolate chunks, the nuts and half the remaining dark chocolate chunks. The mixture will feel quite soft.
2 Drop big spoonfuls in 12 piles on to 2 or 3 baking sheets, leaving room for them to spread. Stick 2–3 pieces of the remaining dark chocolate chunks into each cookie.
3 Bake for 10–12 minutes until they are tinged very slightly darker around the edges. They will be soft in the middle, but will crisp up as they cool. Cook for longer and you'll have crisper cookies. Leave to cool for a few minutes, then transfer to a wire rack.

• Per cookie 381 kcalories, protein 7g, carbohydrate 36g, fat 24g, saturated fat 10g, fibre 2g, added sugar 27g, salt 0.42g

*Creamed coconut adds richness and flavour
to these American-style cookies.*

Coconut and Cashew Cookies

140g/5oz unsalted cashews, toasted
85g/3oz creamed coconut, grated
175g/6oz plain flour
½ tsp baking powder
140g/5oz butter, softened
125g/4½oz dark muscovado sugar
1 tbsp ground ginger
1 egg

Takes 35 minutes • Makes 14–16

1 Preheat the oven to 180ºC/Gas 4/fan oven 160ºC. Split some cashews in half; leave the rest whole. Mix with the coconut and set aside.
2 Blend the remaining ingredients in a food processor to make a smooth, stiff consistency. Set aside four tablespoonfuls of the nut mixture; stir the rest into the flour mixture.
3 Put 14–16 heaped tablespoons of the mixture in mounds, well apart, on buttered baking sheets. Flatten slightly with your fingers. Sprinkle with the reserved nut mixture and bake for 10–12 minutes until golden and set at the edges. Leave for a few minutes, then cool on a rack. The cookies will stay fresh for up to 1 week in an airtight container.

• Per cookie (for fourteen) 262 kcalories, protein 4g, carbohydrate 22g, fat 18g, saturated fat 9g, fibre 2g, added sugar 9g, salt 0.34g

Make these treats for your next birthday party –
for kids or adults.

Smarties Cookies

100g/4oz butter, softened
100g/4oz light muscovado sugar
1 tbsp golden syrup
150g/6oz self-raising flour
85g/3oz Smarties (about 3 tubes)

Takes 20 minutes • Makes 14

1 Preheat the oven to 180°C/Gas 4/fan oven 160°C. Beat the butter and sugar in a bowl until light and creamy, then beat in the syrup.
2 Work in half the flour. Stir in the Smarties with the remaining flour and work the dough together with your fingers. Divide into 14 balls. Place them well apart on baking sheets. Do not flatten them.
3 Bake for 12 minutes until pale golden at the edges. Cool on a wire rack. These cookies will keep for up to 4 days in an airtight tin.

• Per cookie 167 kcalories, protein 2g, carbohydrate 23g, fat 8g, saturated fat 5g, fibre trace, added sugar 13g, salt 0.3g

Store any uncooked mixture in the fridge for up to 1 week, or freeze on the day for up to 6 months, defrosting before baking.

Oaty Cherry Cookies

250g/9oz butter, softened
50g/2oz caster sugar
100g/3½oz light muscovado sugar
150g/5½oz self-raising flour
225g/8oz porridge oats
200g/7oz glacé cherries
50g/2oz raisins

Takes 30 minutes • Makes 18

1 Preheat the oven to 180°C/Gas 4/fan oven 160°C. Line 2 or 3 baking sheets with non-stick baking paper (or bake in batches). In a bowl, beat the butter and sugars together until light and fluffy. Stir in the flour and oats and mix well. Roughly chop three quarters of the cherries, then stir these and the whole cherries and raisins into the oat mixture.

2 Divide the mixture into 18 equal portions. Roughly shape each portion into a ball. Put on the baking sheets well apart to allow for spreading. Lightly flatten each biscuit with your fingertips, keeping the mixture quite rough-looking.

3 Bake for 15–20 minutes until the cookies are pale golden around the edges, but still feel soft in the centre. Cool on the baking sheets for 5 minutes, then transfer to a wire rack.

• Per cookie 249 kcalories, protein 2g, carbohydrate 33g, fat 13g, saturated fat 7g, fibre 1g, added sugar 15g, salt 0.36g

Swap the sultanas for chopped nuts or other dried fruit to vary the recipe for these American-style cookies.

Lemon and Sultana Cookies

350g/12oz plain flour
½ tsp baking powder
½ tsp bicarbonate of soda
140g/5oz butter, cut into small pieces
175g/6oz caster sugar
85g/3oz sultanas
100g/4oz lemon curd
2 eggs, beaten

FOR THE ICING
100g/4oz sifted icing sugar
2 tbsp fresh lemon juice

Takes 30 minutes • Makes 30

1 Preheat the oven to 200ºC/Gas 6/fan oven 180ºC. Butter 3 baking sheets (or bake in several batches). Sift the flour, baking powder and bicarbonate of soda into a bowl. Add the butter and rub in with your fingertips until the mixture resembles fine breadcrumbs.
2 Stir in the sugar and sultanas, add the lemon curd and eggs and mix to a soft dough. Shape the dough into 30 small balls, about 2.5cm/1in wide, and put on the baking sheets, allowing plenty of space between them so they can spread. Using your fingers, gently press the top of each biscuit to flatten it slightly.
3 Bake for 12–15 minutes until risen and light golden. Leave to cool for 1 minute on the baking sheets, then transfer to a wire rack to cool completely. Blend the icing sugar and lemon juice, then drizzle over each cookie.

• Per cookie 134 kcalories, protein 2g, carbohydrate 23g, fat 5g, saturated fat 3g, fibre trace, added sugar 11g, salt 0.2g

Traditionally made with vegetable shortening, this old-fashioned type of cookie dough can also be made into a case for a fruit tart.

Pine Nut Cookies

50g/2oz pine nuts, plus a few extra
175g/6oz butter, softened
140g/5oz golden granulated sugar, plus extra for sprinkling
seeds from 1 star anise, crushed (optional)
1 egg
250g/9oz plain flour
1 tsp baking powder

Takes 1 hour • Makes 18

1 Toast the pine nuts in a dry, heavy-based pan for 1–2 minutes. Set aside.
2 Put the butter, sugar and star anise seeds, if using, in a food processor and whizz for 1 minute. Scrape down the bowl, then whizz again briefly. Add the egg and whizz again. Tip in the flour and baking powder and whizz until the mixture forms a dough. Mix in the pine nuts (reserving enough for step 3), then chill for 30 minutes, wrapped in plastic film.
3 Preheat the oven to 180°C/Gas 4/fan oven 160°C. Take walnut-sized pieces of dough and press out into 5cm/2in rounds, level but not too neat. Put on the baking sheets and press two pine nuts on the top of each. Bake for 15 minutes until pale golden. Transfer to a wire rack to cool, sprinkle with sugar and serve.

• Per cookie 176 kcalories, protein 2g, carbohydrate 20g, fat 10g, saturated fat 5g, fibre trace, added sugar 9g, salt 0.28g

Serve with ripe Taleggio or another soft cheese, such as dolcelatte or St Andre, and a brimming bowl of fresh, juicy strawberries.

Walnut Oat Biscuits

100g/4oz butter, softened
85g/3oz light muscovado sugar
1 egg, beaten
50g/2oz porridge oats
50g/2oz walnuts, finely chopped
85g/3oz plain flour
½ tsp baking powder
cheese and strawberries, to serve

Takes 25 minutes • Makes 15

1 Preheat the oven to 180°C/Gas 4/fan oven 160°C. Butter two baking sheets. In a bowl, beat the butter and sugar for 5 minutes by hand or 2 minutes in the food processor until light and fluffy. Beat in the egg, then stir in the oats, nuts, flour and baking powder.
2 Drop dessertspoonfuls of the mixture, with a little space between, on the baking sheets. Bake for 15 minutes until pale golden, then cool on a wire rack.
3 Serve as described above with the cheese and strawberries. The biscuits will keep fresh in a sealed container for up to a week.

• Per biscuit 133 kcalories, protein 2g, carbohydrate 13g, fat 9g, saturated fat 4g, fibre 1g, added sugar 6g, salt 0.15g

Eat these moreish cookies while they're still warm – that way
the chocolate is still gorgeously gooey in the middle.

Chunky Choc Orange Cookies

250g/9oz butter, softened
50g/2oz caster sugar
100g/3½oz light muscovado sugar
300g/10oz self-raising flour
2 tbsp milk
175g/6oz orange-flavoured dark
chocolate, very roughly chopped
50g/2oz pecan nuts, very roughly
chopped

Takes 30 minutes • Makes 18

1 Preheat the oven to 180º/Gas 4/fan oven 160ºC. Line 2 or 3 baking sheets with non-stick baking paper (or bake in batches). In a bowl, beat together the butter and sugars until light and fluffy. Stir in the flour and milk, mix well, then stir in the chocolate and nuts.
2 Divide the mixture into 18 equal portions. Roughly shape each portion into a ball. Put on the baking sheets well apart to allow for spreading. Lightly flatten each biscuit with your fingertips, keeping the mixture quite rough-looking.
3 Bake for 15–20 minutes until the cookies are pale golden around the edges, but still feel soft in the centre. Cool on the baking sheets for 5 minutes, then transfer to a wire rack and allow to cool a little more before eating.

• Per cookie 261 kcalories, protein 2g, carbohydrate 28g, fat 16g, saturated fat 9g, fibre 1g, added sugar 14g, salt 0.42g

*Light biscuits with a surprise almond filling
and orange-scented sugar.*

Festive Almond Biscuits

75g/3oz unsalted butter, chilled and
cut into pieces
115g/4oz self-raising flour
75g/3oz ground almonds
100g/4oz caster sugar
50g/2oz marzipan, cut into 20 cubes

FOR THE ORANGE SUGAR
pared rind of 2 oranges
50g/2oz icing sugar

Takes 1¼ hours • Makes 20

1 Whizz the butter with the flour and almonds to a breadcrumb consistency. Add half the caster sugar; whizz until the mixture starts to cling together, then work lightly into a ball.
2 Thinly roll out half of the dough. Use 6cm/2½in cutters to cut out crescents and stars; put 20 on a buttered baking sheet. Roll the marzipan cubes into sausage- or ball-shaped pieces and lay on the crecents and stars. Top each with matching dough shape and seal the edges. Chill for 30 minutes.
3 Preheat the oven to 160ºC/Gas 3/fan oven 150ºC. Put the orange rind on a baking sheet and bake for 3 minutes; cool. Mix the remaining caster sugar and the icing sugar; toss with the rind. Bake the biscuits for 18–20 minutes; cool on a wire rack. Sprinkle with the orange sugar.

• Per biscuit 109 kcalories, protein 1g, carbohydrate 14g, fat 6g, saturated fat 2g, fibre 1g, added sugar 9g, salt 0.06g

These delicious biscuits were made to send to the ANZACs (Australian and New Zealand Army Corps) serving in Gallipoli.

Anzac Biscuits

85g/3oz porridge oats
85g/3oz desiccated coconut
100g/4oz plain flour
100g/4oz caster sugar
100g/4oz butter, melted
1 tbsp golden syrup
1 tsp bicarbonate of soda

Takes 35 minutes • Makes 20

1 Preheat the oven to 180ºC/Gas 4/fan oven 160ºC. Put the oats, coconut, flour and sugar in a bowl. Melt the butter in a small pan or microwave and stir in the golden syrup. Add the bicarbonate of soda to 2 tablespoons boiling water, then stir into the golden syrup and butter mixture.
2 Make a well in the middle of the dry ingredients and pour in the butter and golden syrup mixture. Stir gently to incorporate the dry ingredients.
3 Put dessertspoonfuls of the mixture on to buttered baking sheets, about 2.5cm/1in apart to allow room for spreading. Bake in batches for 8–10 minutes until golden. Transfer to a wire rack to cool.

• Per biscuit 118 kcalories, protein 1g, carbohydrate 13g, fat 7g, saturated fat 5g, fibre 1g, added sugar 6g, salt 0.28g

Index

Picture credits and recipe credits

BBC Worldwide would like to thank the following for providing photographs. While every effort has been made to trace and acknowledge all photographers, we would like to apologize should there be any errors or omissions.

Marie-Louise Avery p30, p44, p82, p142, p144, p146, p156, p194; Steve Baxter p138; Martin Brigdale p14, p64, p118; Linda Burgess p24, p38, p46, p66, p72, p100, p108, p140; Jean Cazals p200; Gus Filgate p210; Anna Hodgson p136; David Munns p10, p56, p60, p68, p114, p170, p176; Myles New p18; Michael Paul p26, p28, p84, p98, p104, p132, p162, p166, p192; Craig Robertson p6, p36, p50; Howard Shooter p12; Simon Smith p102, p208;

Simon Smith/Adrian Taylor p168; Roger Stowell p42, p52, p54, p62, p74, p92, p116, p124, p160, p188, p202, p204; Adrian Taylor/Bill Reavell/ Niall McDiarmid p22; Martin Thompson p128; Ian Wallace p16; Philip Webb p32, p34, p40, p58, p76, p80, p88, p106, p112, p152, p164, p172, p178, p184, p186, p190; Simon Wheeler p20, p78, p86, p110, p122, p130, p134, p150, p154, p158, p182, p198, p206; Jonathan Whittaker p148; Geoff Wilkinson p48, p90, p94, p126, p174; Tim Young p70, p96, p120, p180, p196.

Thanks also to the contributors to *BBC Good Food Magazine* and the editorial team, who created the recipes in this book.

Sue Ashworth, Barbara Baker, Lorna Brash, Sara Buenfeld, Mary Cadogan, Jane Clarke, Linda Collister, Alison Cork, Roz Denny, Barney Desmazery, Matthew Drennan, Lewis Esson, Joanna Farrow, Margaret Fineran, Silvana Franco, Moyra Fraser, Brian Glover, Carole Handslip, Alastair Hendy, Margaret Hickey, Carrie Hill, Geraldene Holt, Fiona Hunter, Sue Lawrence, Kate Moseley, Orlando Murrin, Vicky Musselman, Jane Newdick, Angela Nilson, Maggie Pannell, Thane Prince, Rosie Squire, Sue Style, Jenny White, Mitzie Wilson, Antony Worrall Thompson and Jeni Wright.